STUDY GUIDE AND WORKING PAPERS CHAPTERS 13–25

COLLEGE ACCOUNTING
A Practical Approach

Twelfth Edition

Jeffrey Slater
North Shore Community College
Danvers, Massacusetts

PEARSON

Boston   Columbus   Indianapolis   New York   San Francisco   Upper Saddle River
Amsterdam   Cape Town   Dubai   London   Madrid   Milan   Munich   Paris   Montreal   Toronto
Delhi   Mexico City   Sao Paulo   Sydney   Hong Kong   Seoul   Singapore   Taipei   Tokyo

VP/Editorial Director: Sally Yagan
Acquisitions Editor: Lacey Vitetta
Development Editor: Mignon Tucker
Editorial Project Managers: Nicole Sam and Christina Rumbaugh
Editorial Assistants: Jane Avery and Lauren Zanedis
Director of Marketing: Maggie Moylan Leen
Marketing Assistants: Ian Gold and Kimberly Lovato
Senior Managing Editor: Nancy Fenton
Senior Production Project Manager: Roberta Sherman

Manufacturing Buyer: Carol Melville
Cover Designer: Anthony Gemmellaro
Media Project Manager: Sarah Peterson
Media Project Manager, Production: John Cassar
Full-Service Project Management: GEX Publishing Services
Composition: GEX Publishing Services
Printer/Binder: Courier/Kendallville
Cover Printer: Lehigh-Phoenix Color/Hagerstown
Text Font: Times Roman 10/12

Contents

ACCOUNTING FOR BAD DEBTS

INSTANT REPLAY: SELF-REVIEW QUIZ 13-1

1. _____ 2. _____ 3. _____ 4. _____ 5. _____

INSTANT REPLAY: SELF-REVIEW QUIZ 13-2

Name _____ Class _____ Date _____

1. _____ 2. _____ 3. _____ 4. _____ 5. _____

CONCEPT CHECK

1. A.

Account	Category	↑ ↓	Rule
Bad Debt Expense			
Allowance for Doubtful Accounts			

    B. _____
        _____

    C. _____
        _____

2. A. _____
    B. _____
    C. _____
    D. _____

3.

4.

5.

Name _____ Class _____ Date _____

FORMS FOR EXERCISES A or B

13A-1 OR 13B-1

HAMLET.COM
PARTIAL BALANCE SHEET
DECEMBER 31, 2012

13A-2 OR 13B-2

13A-3 OR 13B-3

FORMS FOR EXERCISES A or B

EXERCISES (CONCLUDED)

13A-4 OR 13B-4

(A)

(B)

13A-5 OR 13B-5

END OF CHAPTER PROBLEMS

PROBLEM 13A-1 OR PROBLEM 13B-1

LONG.COM
GENERAL JOURNAL

PAGE 3

Date	Account Titles and Description	PR	Dr.	Cr.

PROBLEM 13A-2 OR PROBLEM 13B-2

LAKE CO.
GENERAL JOURNAL

Date	Account Titles and Description	PR	Dr.	Cr.

LAKE CO.
PARTIAL BALANCE SHEET
DECEMBER 31, 2012

PROBLEM 13A-3 OR PROBLEM 13B-3

T.J. RACE
GENERAL JOURNAL

PAGE 4

Date	Account Titles and Description	PR	Dr.	Cr.

PROBLEM 13A-4 OR PROBLEM 13B-4

SIGMUND COMPANY
GENERAL JOURNAL

Date	Account Titles and Description	PR	Dr.	Cr.

PROBLEM 13A-4 OR PROBLEM 13B-4 (CONTINUED)

SIGMUND COMPANY
GENERAL JOURNAL

Date	Account Titles and Description	PR	Dr.	Cr.

PROBLEM 13A-4 OR PROBLEM 13B-4 (CONTINUED)

ALLOWANCE FOR DOUBTFUL ACCOUNTS   ACCOUNT NO. 114

Date	Explanation	Post Ref.	Debit	Credit	Balance Debit	Balance Credit

INCOME SUMMARY   ACCOUNT NO. 312

Date	Explanation	Post Ref.	Debit	Credit	Balance Debit	Balance Credit

BAD DEBTS EXPENSE   ACCOUNT NO. 612

Date	Explanation	Post Ref.	Debit	Credit	Balance Debit	Balance Credit

PROBLEM 13A-4 OR PROBLEM 13B-4 (CONCLUDED)

SIGMUND COMPANY
PARTIAL BALANCE SHEET
DECEMBER 31, 2012

CHAPTER 13
SUMMARY PRACTICE TEST
ACCOUNTING FOR BAD DEBTS

Part I Instructions

Fill in the blank(s) to complete the statement.

1. _____ _____ could be estimated based on percentage of sales.

2. The _____ _____ _____ uses aging of accounts receivable.

3. _____ _____ _____ equals Accounts Receivable less Allowance for Doubtful Accounts.

4. When writing off an account in the allowance method, the account _____ _____ _____ is not involved.

5. In the allowance method, to estimate bad debts you may use either the _____ _____ or the _____ _____ approach.

6. In the income statement approach, any existing balance in the Allowance for Doubtful Accounts is _____.

7. _____ _____ _____ _____ classifies customers' accounts according to days past due.

8. The _____ _____ _____ method does not match accrual accounting.

9. _____ _____ _____ is a revenue account found in the other income section of an income statement.

10. An unusual balance in the _____ _____ _____ _____ indicates that the estimate for bad debts was too low.

Part II Instructions

Answer true or false to the following.

1. Allowance for doubtful accounts is recorded on the income statement.

2. The direct method has no allowance account.

3. The direct method follows the matching principle.

4. The normal balance of Allowance for Doubtful Accounts is a credit.

5. In the direct method, the account Bad Debts Recovered is used when an account is reinstated only in the same year the sale is made.

6. When an account is written off in the allowance method, Bad Debts Expense is debited.

7. The balance sheet approach of estimating bad debts using the allowance method will adjust the balance in the allowance account.

8. Net Realizable Value equals Accounts Receivable plus the Allowance for Doubtful Accounts.

9. The direct write-off method requires the allowance account.

10. Bad Debts Expense is found on the income statement.

11. In the direct method, Accounts Receivable is recorded at net.

12. The income statement approach may estimate Bad Debts Expense on a percent of net credit sales.

13. Aging the Accounts Receivable can only be used in the direct write-off method.

14. A debit to Bad Debts Expense and a credit to the Allowance for Doubtful Accounts means a customer's account has been declared uncollectible.

15. Using the allowance method, a debit to Allowance for Doubtful Accounts and a credit to Accounts Receivable means that an accounts receivable is thought to be uncollectible.

16. Using the direct write-off method, a debit to Bad Debts Expense and a credit to Accounts Receivable means a customer's account is thought to be uncollectible.

17. A debit to Accounts Receivable and a credit to Bad Debts Recovered means that a bad debt has been recovered in the same year as the sale.

18. The direct write-off method does not show net realized value.

19. Net realizable value is recorded on the income statement.

20. The Direct Write-off Method is really part of the allowance method.

CHAPTER 13
SOLUTIONS TO SUMMARY PRACTICE TEST

Part I

1. Bad debts
2. balance sheet approach
3. Net Realizable Value
4. Bad Debts Expense
5. income statement; balance sheet

6. ignored
7. Aging the accounts receivable
8. direct write-off
9. Bad Debts Recovered
10. Allowance for Doubtful Accounts

Part II

1. false
2. true
3. false
4. true
5. false
6. false
7. true
8. false
9. false
10. true

11. false
12. true
13. false
14. false
15. true
16. true
17. false
18. true
19. false
20. false

CONTINUING PROBLEM—ON THE JOB FOR CHAPTER 13

GENERAL JOURNAL

PAGE 2

Date		Account Titles and Description	PR	Dr.				Cr.			

NOTES RECEIVABLE AND NOTES PAYABLE

INSTANT REPLAY: SELF-REVIEW QUIZ 14-1

Name _____ Class _____ Date _____

INSTANT REPLAY: SELF-REVIEW QUIZ 14-2

Name _____ Class _____ Date _____

INSTANT REPLAY: SELF-REVIEW QUIZ 14-3

(A)

Step 1

Step 2

Step 3

Step 4

(B, C)

INSTANT REPLAY: SELF-REVIEW QUIZ 14-4

1. _____   2. _____   3. _____   4. _____   5. _____

CONCEPT CHECK

1. A. _____
_____

    B. _____

2. A. _____
_____

    B. _____
_____

3.

4. _____
_____
_____
_____

5. _____
_____
_____
_____
_____
_____
_____
_____

CONCEPT CHECK (CONTINUED)

6.

7.

8. ACCOUNTS AFFECTED | CATEGORY | ↑ ↓ | DR. or CR. | AMOUNT

ACCOUNTS AFFECTED	CATEGORY	↑ ↓	DR. or CR.	AMOUNT

9.

FORMS FOR EXERCISES A or B

14A-1 OR 14B-1

A. _____

B. _____

C. _____

14A-2 OR 14B-2

A. _____

_____

B. _____

_____

_____

_____

C. _____

D. _____

_____

_____

_____

14A-3 OR 14B-3.

A. _____

_____

_____

B. _____

_____

_____

C. _____

D. _____

_____

_____

EXERCISES (CONCLUDED)

14A-4 OR 14B-4

1. _____
   _____

2. _____
   _____
   _____
   _____

3. _____
   _____

4. _____
   _____

A.

14A-5 OR 14B-5

_____
_____
_____

END OF CHAPTER PROBLEMS

PROBLEM 14A-1 OR PROBLEM 14B-1

GENERAL JOURNAL

PAGE 1

Date	Account Titles and Description	PR	Dr.	Cr.

PROBLEM 14A-1 OR PROBLEM 14B-1 (CONCLUDED)

GENERAL JOURNAL

PAGE 2

Date	Account Titles and Description	PR	Dr.	Cr.

PROBLEM 14A-2 OR PROBLEM 14B-2

MARCUS CO.
GENERAL JOURNAL

Date		Account Titles and Description	PR	Dr.	Cr.

PROBLEM 14A-3 OR PROBLEM 14B-3

JONES CO.
GENERAL JOURNAL

PAGE 2

Date	Account Titles and Description	PR	Dr.	Cr.

PROBLEM 14A-4 OR PROBLEM 14B-4

ALDEN COMPANY
GENERAL JOURNAL

PAGE 2

Date	Account Titles and Description	PR	Dr.	Cr.

PROBLEM 14A-4 OR PROBLEM 14B-4 (CONCLUDED)

ALDEN COMPANY
GENERAL JOURNAL

PAGE 3

Date	Account Titles and Description	PR	Dr.	Cr.

CHAPTER 14
SUMMARY PRACTICE TEST:
NOTES RECEIVABLE AND NOTES PAYABLE

Part I Instructions

Fill in the blank(s) to complete the statement.

1. Formal written promises result in _____ _____.

2. The _____ is the person or company to whom a promissory note is payable.

3. _____ _____ is classified on the income statement as other expense.

4. _____ represents the face value or amount stated on the note indicating the amount borrowed.

5. _____ _____ is a current asset on the balance sheet.

6. A(n) _____ _____ for a buyer means a shifting of an accounts payable to a notes payable.

7. If a buyer fails to pay the maturity value, the note is said to be _____.

8. A seller's Interest Income would be a buyer's _____ _____.

9. _____ is a way of exchanging a note for cash before the maturity date.

10. The amount a company receives from a note that is discounted before the maturity date is called the _____.

11. The amount the bank charges in discounting a note before the maturity date is called the _____ _____.

12. The number of days from the date of discounting until the maturity date is called the _____ period.

13. One who discounts a note may be _____ _____ if the maker of the note defaults at maturity date.

14. A contra account involving notes would be _____ _____ _____ _____.

15. _____ _____ _____ represents income that has been earned during the period but has not been received or recorded because payment is not yet due.

Part II Instructions

Match the term in the column on the left to the definition, example, or phrase in the column on the right. Be sure to use a letter only once.

___e___	**1.** EXAMPLE: Maker	a. when notes comes due
_____	**2.** payee	b. current liability on balance sheet
_____	**3.** Notes Receivable	c. effective rate
_____	**4.** Proceeds	d. dishonored
_____	**5.** The true rate of simple interest	e. one who will pay a promissory note
_____	**6.** Discount on Notes Payable	f. debit
_____	**7.** Maturity date	g. discounting one's own note
_____	**8.** Normal balance of discount on notes payable	h. amount due from formal written promises
		i. party to whom note is payable
_____	**9.** Adjustment for interest income	j. credit
_____	**10.** Principal and interest	k. could be reversed
_____	**11.** Normal balance of Notes Payable	l. maturity value—bank discount
_____	**12.** Notes Payable	m. interest incurred, not yet paid or recorded, since payment not yet due
_____	**13.** Accrued interest	
_____	**14.** Not paid at maturity	n. contra liability
		o. maturity value

Part III Instructions

Answer true or false to the following.

1. Discount on Notes Payable does not record interest deducted in advance.

2. The normal balance of Discount on Notes Payable is a credit.

3. Adjustment for accrued interest must be reversed at the start of a new year.

4. Interest-bearing notes cannot overlap different accounting periods.

5. Proceeds = Maturity Value – Bank Discount.

6. Maturity value is always principal plus interest.

7. Contingent liability means that the one discounting the note has no further liability.

8. A protest fee could result if a note is dishonored at maturity.

9. An endorsement without recourse could result in one having contingent liability.

10. The proceeds of a note can never be less than the maturity value.

11. Bank Discount = MV times Bank Discount Rate times 360.

12. The discount period represents the number of days the bank holds the note until maturity.

13. The process of discounting results in the exchange of a note for another note.

14. Interest Income is reported on the balance sheet.

15. Only unmatured notes are in the Notes Receivable account.

16. Subsidiary ledgers are required for Notes Receivable and Payable.

17. Notes Payable is always a long-term liability on the balance sheet.

18. The maturity date of a note can be determined by tables.

19. There are 92 days between June 1 and September 1.

20. All interest calculations must use 360 days.

CHAPTER 14
SOLUTIONS TO SUMMARY PRACTICE TEST

Part I

1. promissory notes
2. payee
3. Interest Expense
4. Principal
5. Notes Receivable
6. time extension
7. dishonored
8. Interest Expense
9. Discounting
10. proceeds
11. bank discount
12. discount
13. contingently liable
14. Discount on Notes Payable
15. Accrued Interest Income

Part II

1. e
2. i
3. h
4. l
5. c
6. n
7. a
8. f
9. k
10. o
11. j
12. b
13. m
14. d

Part III

1.	false	11.	false
2.	false	12.	true
3.	false	13.	false
4.	false	14.	false
5.	true	15.	true
6.	false	16.	false
7.	false	17.	false
8.	true	18.	true
9.	false	19.	true
10.	false	20.	false

CONTINUING PROBLEM—ON THE JOB FOR CHAPTER 14

_____

_____

_____

_____

_____

_____

_____

ACCOUNTING FOR MERCHANDISE INVENTORY

15

INSTANT REPLAY: SELF-REVIEW QUIZ 15-1

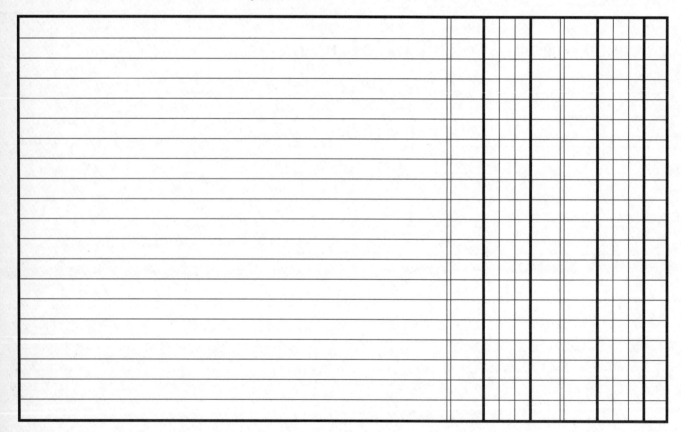

INSTANT REPLAY: SELF-REVIEW QUIZ 15-2

(1)

Merchandise Inventory   114

INVENTORY ITEM _____

Date	Purchased	Sold	Balance

INVENTORY ITEM _____

Date			

Name _____ Class _____ Date _____

INSTANT REPLAY: SELF-REVIEW QUIZ 15-3

1. _____
_____
_____
_____
_____
_____
_____
_____
_____
_____
_____
_____
_____
_____
_____
_____
_____
_____
_____
_____
_____
_____
_____
_____
_____
_____
_____
_____
_____
_____
_____
_____

2. a. _____   b. _____   c. _____

INSTANT REPLAY: SELF-REVIEW QUIZ 15-4

1.

	Cost	Retail

2.   a. _____   b. _____   c. _____   d. _____   e. _____

CHAPTER 15
CONCEPT CHECK

1.

2.

GENERAL JOURNAL

Date 201X		Account Titles and Description	PR		Dr.		Cr.	

CONCEPT CHECK (CONTINUED)

3.

GENERAL JOURNAL

Date 201X		Account Titles and Description	PR		Dr.		Cr.

4.

GENERAL JOURNAL

Date 201X		Account Titles and Description	PR		Dr.		Cr.

Name _____ Class _____ Date _____

CONCEPT CHECK (CONTINUED)

5.

_____

_____

_____

_____

_____

_____

_____

_____

_____

_____

_____

_____

_____

_____

_____

_____

_____

_____

_____

_____

_____

_____

_____

_____

_____

_____

_____

_____

_____

_____

_____

CONCEPT CHECK (CONCLUDED)

6. A. _____
   B. _____
   C. _____
   D. _____
   E. _____
   _____
   _____
   _____

7. A. _____
   B. _____
   C. _____
   D. _____

FORMS FOR EXERCISES A or B

15A-1 OR 15B-1

LANE ELECTRIC CO.
GENERAL JOURNAL

				Dr.		Cr.	

15A-2 OR 15B-2

Inventory Report Form   Item _____

Date	Purchased	Sold	Balance

EXERCISES (CONTINUED)

15A-3 OR 15B-3   PAGE 1

Cash	111		Accounts Payable	201

Merchandise Inventory	114		Sales	401

Cost of Goods Sold	501

Name _____ Class _____ Date _____

EXERCISES (CONTINUED)

15A-4 OR 15B-4 (Use blank inventory control card.)   Inventory Item _____

Date	Received			Sold			Balance		
	Units	Cost	Total	Units	Cost	Total	Units	Cost	Total

15A-5 OR 15B-5

_____
_____
_____
_____
_____
_____

FIFO
_____
_____
_____
_____
_____

LIFO
_____
_____
_____
_____
_____

Weighted Average
_____
_____
_____
_____

EXERCISES (CONCLUDED)

15A-6 OR 15B-6

15A-7 OR 15B-7 Retail Method

15A-8 OR 15B-8 Gross Profit Method

END OF CHAPTER PROBLEMS

PROBLEM 15A-1 OR PROBLEM 15B-1

ALTON CO.
GENERAL JOURNAL

PAGE 3

Date			PR	Dr.	Cr.

PROBLEM 15A-2 OR PROBLEM 15B-2

SALEM ELECTRONICS
GENERAL JOURNAL

PAGE 2

Date	Account Titles and Description	PR	Dr.	Cr.

PROBLEM 15A-2 OR PROBLEM 15B-2 (CONTINUED)

Inventory Item _____

Date	Received			Sold			Balance		
	Units	Cost	Total	Units	Cost	Total	Units	Cost	Total

Inventory Item _____

Date	Received			Sold			Balance		
	Units	Cost	Total	Units	Cost	Total	Units	Cost	Total

Inventory Item _____

Date	Received			Sold			Balance		
	Units	Cost	Total	Units	Cost	Total	Units	Cost	Total

PROBLEM 15A-2 OR PROBLEM 15B-2 (CONTINUED)

GENERAL LEDGER

CASH **ACCOUNT NO. 101**

Date	Explanation	Post Ref.	Debit	Credit	Balance Debit	Credit

MERCHANDISE INVENTORY **ACCOUNT NO. 114**

Date	Explanation	Post Ref.	Debit	Credit	Balance Debit	Credit

ACCOUNTS PAYABLE **ACCOUNT NO. 201**

Date	Explanation	Post Ref.	Debit	Credit	Balance Debit	Credit

SALES **ACCOUNT NO. 401**

Date	Explanation	Post Ref.	Debit	Credit	Balance Debit	Credit

Name _____ Class _____ Date _____

PROBLEM 15A-2 OR PROBLEM 15B-2 (CONCLUDED)

SALES RETURNS AND ALLOWANCES　　　　**ACCOUNT NO. 402**

Date	Explanation	Post Ref.	Debit	Credit	Balance Debit	Balance Credit

COST OF GOODS SOLD　　　　**ACCOUNT NO. 501**

Date	Explanation	Post Ref.	Debit	Credit	Balance Debit	Balance Credit

Name _____ Class _____ Date _____

PROBLEM 15A-3 OR PROBLEM 15B-3

A. FIFO

	Date	Received			Sold			Balance		
		Units	Cost per Unit	Total	Units	Cost per Unit	Total	Units	Cost per Unit	Total
1.										
2.										
3.										
4.										
5.										
6.										
7.										
8.										
9.										
10.										
11.										
12.										
13.										

B. LIFO

	Date	Received			Sold			Balance		
		Units	Cost per Unit	Total	Units	Cost per Unit	Total	Units	Cost per Unit	Total
1.										
2.										
3.										
4.										
5.										
6.										
7.										
8.										
9.										
10.										
11.										
12.										
13.										

PROBLEM 15A-4 OR PROBLEM 15B-4

PROBLEM 15A-4 OR PROBLEM 15B-4 (CONCLUDED)

PROBLEM 15A-5 OR PROBLEM 15B-5

Name _____ Class _____ Date _____

PROBLEM 15A-6 OR PROBLEM 15B-6

CHAPTER 15
SUMMARY PRACTICE TEST:
ACCOUNTING FOR MERCHANDISE INVENTORY

Part I Instructions

Fill in the blank(s) to complete the statement.

1. In the _____ _____ system, purchases and sales of inventory are recorded in the inventory account.

2. In the _____ _____ system, the inventory account is not updated by each sale or purchase of inventory made during the periods.

3. Cost of goods sold plus _____ _____ equals cost of goods available for sale.

4. _____ _____ _____ is the actual physical movement of how goods are sold for inventory.

5. _____ _____ _____ is determined by what costs are assigned by various inventory methods.

6. Flow of goods and flow of costs are the same in the _____ _____ _____.

7. Using the _____ _____ method, the net income will not fluctuate as much as other methods when the income statement is prepared.

8. In the _____ method, the most recent costs are assigned to goods not sold.

9. The _____ method assumes that the ending inventory is made up of the old inventory.

10. During inflation, LIFO produces the _____ net income.

11. Financial reports are made more reliable by the principle of _____.

12. The _____ principle helps clarify why a company makes a change in the preparation of its financial statements.

13. Consigned goods belong to the _____ and will be added to its inventory.

14. _____ _____ means the seller pays the cost of freight.

15. If beginning inventory is understated, net income will be _____.

Part II Instructions

Match the term in the column on the left to the definition, example, or phrase in the column on the right. Be sure to use a letter only once.

__g__ **1.** Perpetual inventory system

_____ **2.** FIFO

_____ **3.** SUTA

_____ **4.** LIFO

_____ **5.** Petty cash

_____ **6.** OASDI

_____ **7.** Purchases discount

_____ **8.** Controlling account

_____ **9.** Consignee

_____ **10.** NSF

a. Reduces cost of goods sold

b. Improves control of cash

c. Newest units sold first

d. Social security tax

e. A "hot" check

f. Equals total of subsidiary ledger

g. Inventory always up to date

h. Doesn't have ownership

i. Oldest units sold first

j. Unemployment tax

Part III Instructions

Answer true or false to the following.

1. If ending inventory is overstated then COGS is understated.

2. LIFO assumes the old goods are sold first.

3. Sales Returns and Allowances is a contra-revenue account.

4. Net sales less cost of goods sold equals gross profit.

5. In the perpetual system the purchases account is not used.

CHAPTER 15
SOLUTIONS TO SUMMARY PRACTICE TEST

Part I

1. perpetual inventory
2. periodic inventory
3. ending inventory
4. Flow of goods
5. Flow of costs

6. specific invoice method
7. weighted-average
8. FIFO
9. LIFO
10. lowest

11. consistency
12. disclosure
13. consignor
14. FOB Destination
15. overstated

Part II

1. g
2. i
3. j
4. c
5. b

6. d
7. a
8. f
9. h
10. e

Part III

1. true
2. false
3. true
4. true
5. true

Name _____ Class _____ Date _____

CONTINUING PROBLEM—ON THE JOB FOR CHAPTER 15

FIFO

_____
_____
_____
_____
_____

LIFO

_____
_____
_____
_____
_____

WA

_____
_____
_____
_____
_____

Accounting for Property, Plant, Equipment, and Intangible Assets

16

INSTANT REPLAY: SELF-REVIEW QUIZ 16-1

1. _____   2. _____   3. _____   4. _____   5. _____

INSTANT REPLAY: SELF-REVIEW QUIZ 16-2

(A)

END OF YEAR	COST OF EQUIPMENT	YEARLY DEP. EXPENSE	ACC. DEP. END OF YEAR	BOOK VALUE END OF YEAR COST-ACC. DEP.
1.				
2.				
3.				
4.				
5.				

(B)

END OF YEAR	COST OF EQUIPMENT	UNITS OF OUTPUT IN YEAR	YEARLY DEPRECIATION EXPENSE	ACCUMULATED DEPRECIATION END OF YEAR	BOOK VALUE END OF YEAR
1.					
2.					
3.					
4.					
5.					

Name _____ Class _____ Date _____

(C)

END OF YEAR	COST	ACC. DEP. BEG. OF YEAR	BOOK VALUE BEG. OF YEAR (COST-ACC. DEP.)	DEP. EXPENSE (B.V. BEG. OF YEAR X RATE)	ACC. DEP. END OF YEAR	BOOK VALUE END OF YEAR (COST-ACC. DEP.)
1.						
2.						
3.						
4.						
5.						

INSTANT REPLAY: SELF-REVIEW QUIZ 16-3

1. _____ 2. _____ 3. _____ 4. _____ 5. _____
6. _____ 7. _____

INSTANT REPLAY: SELF-REVIEW QUIZ 16-4

1. _____ 2. _____ 3. _____ 4. _____ 5. _____

CONCEPT CHECK

1.

2.

3.

4.

5.

6. A.
   B.
   C.
   D.

7. A.
   B.
   C.

CONCEPT CHECK (CONTINUED)

8. A. _____

_____

_____

_____

B.

9.

10.

Name _____ Class _____ Date _____

FORMS FOR EXERCISES A or B

16A-1 OR 16B-1

_____
_____
_____
_____
_____
_____
_____

16A-2 OR 16B-2

A.   Straight-Line _____
_____
_____
_____
_____
_____

B.   Units-of-Production _____
_____
_____
_____
_____
_____
_____

C.   Declining-Balance _____
_____
_____
_____
_____
_____
_____

Name _____ Class _____ Date _____

EXERCISES (CONTINUED)

16A-3 OR 16B-3
A.   Straight-Line _____

_____
_____
_____
_____
_____
_____

B.   Declining-Balance _____

_____
_____
_____
_____

_____
_____

16A-4 OR 16B-4
_____

A. _____

_____

B. _____

C.

EXERCISES (CONTINUED)

16A-4 OR 16B-4
D. _____

_____

_____

_____

_____

16A-5 OR 16B-5

16A-6 OR 16B-6 _____

_____

_____

_____

_____

_____

END OF CHAPTER PROBLEMS

PROBLEM 16A-1 OR PROBLEM 16B-1

WHITE CO.
GENERAL JOURNAL

PAGE 4

Date	Account Titles and Description	PR	Dr.	Cr.

PROBLEM 16A-2 OR PROBLEM 16B-2

(A)

END OF YEAR	COST OF EQUIPMENT	YEARLY DEP. EXPENSE	ACC. DEP. END OF YEAR	BOOK VALUE END OF YEAR

(B)

END OF YEAR	COST OF EQUIPMENT	UNITS PRODUCED	YEARLY DEPRECIATION EXPENSE	ACCUMULATED DEPRECIATION END OF YEAR	BOOK VALUE END OF YEAR

PROBLEM 16A-2 OR PROBLEM 16B-2 (CONCLUDED)

(C)

END OF YEAR	COST	ACC. DEP. BEG. OF YEAR	BOOK VALUE BEG. OF YEAR	DEPRECIATION EXPENSE	ACC. DEP. END OF YEAR	BOOK VALUE END OF YEAR

PROBLEM 16A-3 OR PROBLEM 16B-3

(A)

END OF YEAR	COST OF EQUIPMENT	YEARLY DEP. EXPENSE	ACC. DEP. END OF YEAR	BOOK VALUE END OF YEAR

(B)

END OF YEAR	COST OF EQUIP.	ACC. DEP. BEG. OF YEAR	BOOK VALUE BEG. OF YEAR	DEPRECIATION EXPENSE	ACC. DEP. END OF YEAR	BOOK VALUE END OF YEAR

Name _____ Class _____ Date _____

PROBLEM 16A-4 OR PROBLEM 16B-4

ROUND CO.
GENERAL JOURNAL   PAGE 3

Date		Account Titles and Description	PR	Dr.	Cr.

PROBLEM 16A-4 OR PROBLEM 16B-4 (CONCLUDED)

Date		Account Titles and Description	PR		Dr.		Cr.	

CHAPTER 16
SUMMARY PRACTICE TEST:
ACCOUNTING FOR PROPERTY, PLANT,
EQUIPMENT, AND INTANGIBLE ASSETS

Part I Instructions

Fill in the blank(s) to complete the statement.

1. _____ _____ _____ is the most used depreciation method today.

2. Oil, timber, and coal are examples of _____ _____.

3. _____ does not depreciate, since it has an indefinite life.

4. _____ is the allocation of costs of plant and equipment assets over their useful life to record the portion of benefits consumed or expired during a specific period.

5. _____ _____ of equipment does not change.

6. _____ _____ is an asset account that records improvement to land with limited useful life.

7. _____ _____ result in an increase in expenses and provide benefits in the current accounting period.

8. Changing tires on a car is an example of a(n) _____ _____.

9. Additions, extraordinary repairs, and betterments are categories of _____ _____.

10. Adding an air conditioner to a car is an example of a(n) _____.

11. Passage of time in the _____ _____ _____ _____ doesn't determine the amount of depreciation taken.

12. _____ _____ is a contra asset.

13. Salvage value is not deducted from calculations from cost in the _____ _____ _____. In this method the asset cannot be depreciated below its salvage value.

14. MACRS allocates depreciation in a much _____ estimated useful life.

15. The loss on disposal account is a(n) _____ _____ on the income statement.

16. A(n) _____ _____ _____ of an asset results if the cash received is greater than the book value.

17. Income tax rules require gains and losses in exchange of assets to be _____ into the cost of a new asset.

18. Loss on exchange of machinery is categorized as a(n) _____ _____ on the income statement.

Name _____ Class _____ Date _____

Part II Instructions

Match the term in the column on the left to the definition, example, or phrase in the column on the right. Be sure to use a letter only once.

___d___   **1.** EXAMPLE: Patents
_____   **2.** Cost of machine
_____   **3.** Equal yearly depreciation
_____   **4.** Not related to passage of time
_____   **5.** Paving a parking lot
_____   **6.** Historical cost
_____   **7.** Income tax method
_____   **8.** Overhauling an engine
_____   **9.** Purchase equipment after the 15th of the month
_____   **10.** Declining-balance
_____   **11.** MACRS
_____   **12.** Grease and oil for a truck
_____   **13.** Original cost remains the same in the calculation
_____   **14.** Gain on sale
_____   **15.** Capital expenditure

a. Extraordinary repair
b. An accelerated method
c. Eliminates concept of useful life
d. Intangible asset.
e. Other income.
f. Freight, assembly, other costs
g. Gains and losses absorbed
h. Land improvement
i. Declining-balance method
j. Straight-line method
k. Units-of-production method
l. Additions, extraordinary repairs, betterments
m. Depreciation disregarded for month
n. original cost
o. Revenue expenditures

Part III Instructions

Answer true or false to the following.

1. Goodwill is equal to the cost of the asset purchased less the value of liabilities identified.
2. Cost of obtaining a franchise is amortized over its life or 40 years, whichever is shorter.
3. Amortization of patents is found in the balance sheet as an operating expense.
4. Accumulated Depletion is a contra asset on the balance sheet.
5. The Internal Revenue Service does recognize gains on exchange of similar assets.
6. A gain when absorbed into the cost of an asset allows for more depreciation in future periods.
7. A loss on exchange of equipment can result if the book value of the old equipment is larger than the trade-in value.
8. In selling a plant asset, a loss results if cash received is less than the book value of assets sold.
9. In the declining-balance method, the equipment may be depreciated below the residual value.
10. MACRS is used for tax reporting, but is not generally acceptable for preparing financial reports.
11. MACRS is not used today.
12. Equipment purchased on June 8 means depreciation is taken as of June 1.
13. Historical cost of assets always changes.
14. In the units-of-production method, depreciation expense is lowest in the last year.
15. A piece of equipment to be depreciated over 10 years by the straight-line method is based on a depreciation rate of 20 percent.
16. Overhauling an airplane is an example of a betterment.

17. A betterment does not extend the life of an asset.
18. Extraordinary repairs will extend the life of an asset.
19. An addition to a high school would be charged to the asset account.
20. The cost of extraordinary repairs is a reduction to accumulated depreciation.

CHAPTER 16
SOLUTIONS TO SUMMARY PRACTICE TEST

Part I

1. Straight-line Depreciation
2. natural resources
3. Land
4. Depreciation
5. Historical cost
6. Land improvement
7. Revenue expenditures
8. revenue expenditure
9. capital expenditures
10. betterment
11. units-of-production method
12. Accumulated Depreciation
13. declining-balance method
14. shorter
15. other expense
16. gain on sale
17. absorbed
18. other expense

Part II

1. d
2. f
3. j
4. k
5. h
6. n
7. g
8. a
9. m
10. b
11. c
12. o
13. i
14. e
15. l

Part III

1. false
2. true
3. false
4. true
5. false
6. false
7. true
8. true
9. false
10. true
11. false
12. true
13. false
14. false
15. false
16. false
17. true
18. true
19. true
20. true

PARTNERSHIPS

INSTANT REPLAY: SELF-REVIEW QUIZ 17-1

1. _____ 2. _____ 3. _____ 4. _____ 5. _____

Name _____ Class _____ Date _____

INSTANT REPLAY: SELF-REVIEW QUIZ 17-2

INSTANT REPLAY: SELF-REVIEW QUIZ 17-3

1. _____	2. _____	3. _____	4. _____	5. _____
6. _____	7. _____	8. _____		

Name _____ Class _____ Date _____

INSTANT REPLAY: SELF-REVIEW QUIZ 17-4

CONCEPT CHECK

1.

2.

3.

4.   Slater   Ring   Flynn

  A. Salary Allow.

  B. Int. on capital invest.

Name _____ Class _____ Date _____

CONCEPT CHECK (CONCLUDED)

5. A. _____
_____
_____
_____

B. _____
_____
_____
_____

6.

7. _____
_____
_____
_____

8. _____
_____
_____
_____

9.

FORMS FOR EXERCISES A or B

17A-1 OR 17B-1

17A-2 OR 17B-2

Interest on Capital
Investments
_____
_____
_____

Net Income
- Interest Allowance
_____
_____

Earnings to Be
Distributed Equally
_____
_____

Share of Net Income
to Partners
_____

17A-3 OR 17B-3

_____
_____
_____
_____

EXERCISES (CONCLUDED)

17A-4 OR 17B-4

17A-5 OR 17B-5

END OF CHAPTER PROBLEMS

PROBLEM 17A-1 OR PROBLEM 17B-1

	CAROL	JACK	TOTALS

Name _____   Class _____   Date _____

PROBLEM 17A-1 OR PROBLEM 17B-1 (CONCLUDED)

	CAROL		JACK		TOTALS	

PROBLEM 17A-2 OR PROBLEM 17B-2

Date		Account Titles and Description	PR		Dr.			Cr.	

PROBLEM 17A-3 OR PROBLEM 17B-3

LRV REPAIR SERVICE
GENERAL JOURNAL

Date	Account Titles and Description	PR	Dr.	Cr.

PROBLEM 17A-4 OR PROBLEM 17B-4

JACKSON, RACKLEY, AND SURBER
GENERAL JOURNAL

PAGE 13

Date		Account Titles and Description	PR		Dr.			Cr.	

PROBLEM 17A-4 OR PROBLEM 17B-4 (CONCLUDED)

JACKSON, RACKLEY, AND SURBER
GENERAL JOURNAL

PAGE 14

Date	Account Titles and Description	PR	Dr.	Cr.

CHAPTER 17
SUMMARY PRACTICE TEST:
PARTNERSHIPS

Part I Instructions

Fill in the blank(s) to complete the statement.

1. Many law offices are _____.

2. The _____ _____ _____ is a written agreement that formalizes the partners' relationship.

3. _____ _____ occurs when a partner, acting in the normal scope of business, enters into a contract that binds each of the partners.

4. _____ _____ is based on personal service.

5. When partners invest in the business, the assets should be recorded at their _____ _____ _____.

6. Partners work for the partnership's _____ and not for a salary.

7. If an agreement is not made on how partners share earnings, they will be divided _____.

8. _____ _____ _____ _____ is a way to divide up earnings in a partnership.

9. Earnings of a partnership are closed to Income Summary and each partner's _____ _____.

10. A(n) _____ may result to other partners if an incoming partner has to pay more than what his or her equity is worth.

11. A bonus to old partners would be shared in their _____ _____ _____ ratio.

12. _____ or _____ of a partner means a new partnership must be formed.

13. The process of converting assets into cash and paying off obligations and equity is called _____.

14. One partner cannot _____ another partner to accept a new partner.

15. The _____ _____ _____ _____ is a supporting document that calculates the ending capital balance for each partner.

Part II Instructions

Match the term in the column on the left to the definition, example, or phrase in the column on the right. Be sure to use a letter only once.

__g__	1. EXAMPLE: Articles of partnership	**a.**	Unlimited liability
_____	2. Pay more than equity interest	**b.**	Act binding on each partner
_____	3. Limited life	**c.**	Current fair value
_____	4. Two or more co-owners	**d.**	Not an expense
_____	5. Capital is updated	**e.**	Bonus to old partners
_____	6. Partners invest in business	**f.**	Closing
_____	7. Divide up earnings	**g.**	Written contract spelling out details of partnership
_____	8. Interest Allowance	**h.**	Salary and interest
_____	9. Ratio	**i.**	Assets sold, liabilities, and partners paid
_____	10. Admission of a new partner	**j.**	Deficit
_____	11. General partner	**k.**	3:3:2
_____	12. Shared equally	**l.**	Dissolved by admission, withdrawal, or death
_____	13. Negative balance	**m.**	Buy equity, make an investment
_____	14. Liquidation	**n.**	No agreement
_____	15. Mutual agency	**o.**	Partnership

Part III Instructions

Answer true or false to the following.

1. Salary allowance cannot be used in partnerships.
2. Interest allowance cannot be based on percent of partners' capital balances.
3. The statement of partners' equity calculates the ending capital balance that will be found on the income statement.
4. Forming a partnership must be done in written form.
5. When a partnership is formed, assets are recorded at their current fair value.
6. A partnership lasts for only 10 years.
7. Mutual agency might bind the partners of a business based on the act of one partner who entered into a contract as an agent of the company.
8. A partner may withdraw more or less than the salary allowance.
9. Liquidation means selling part of the assets to pay off a creditor.
10. A bonus is paid in a partnership only if a company earns large profits.
11. A partner can force another partner to accept a new partner.
12. Revaluation of assets is shared based on the profit-and-loss ratio.
13. The first step in the liquidation process is to sell assets for cash.
14. A limited partner has unlimited liability.
15. Salary allowance cannot be used to divide earnings if the partnership is losing money.

Name _____ Class _____ Date _____

16. Ease of formation is a characteristic of partnership.

17. Loss or gain from realization results from the selling of noncash assets in the liquidation process.

18. A partnership can be dissolved but still be in operation.

19. If Bill Jones owns 1/4 equity interest, this means he is entitled to 1/4 of the company's earnings.

20. Physicians cannot form a partnership.

CHAPTER 17
SOLUTIONS TO SUMMARY PRACTICE TEST

Part I

1. partnerships
2. articles of partnership
3. Mutual agency
4. Salary allowance
5. current fair value
6. earnings
7. equally
8. Salary and interest allowance
9. capital account
10. bonus
11. profit-and-loss
12. Withdrawal, death
13. liquidation
14. force
15. statement of partners' equity

Part II

1. g
2. e
3. l
4. o
5. f
6. c
7. h
8. d
9. k
10. m
11. a
12. n
13. j
14. i
15. b

Part III

1. false
2. false
3. false
4. false
5. true
6. false
7. true
8. true
9. false
10. false
11. false
12. true
13. true
14. false
15. false
16. true
17. true
18. true
19. false
20. false

18

CORPORATIONS— ORGANIZATIONS AND STOCK

INSTANT REPLAY: SELF-REVIEW QUIZ 18-1

1. _____   2. _____   3. _____   4. _____   5. _____

INSTANT REPLAY: SELF-REVIEW QUIZ 18-2

1. _____   2. _____   3. _____   4. _____   5. _____   6. _____

INSTANT REPLAY: SELF-REVIEW QUIZ 18-3

(1)

Name_____ Class_____ Date_____

INSTANT REPLAY: SELF-REVIEW QUIZ 18-3 (CONCLUDED)

(2)   PREFERRED   COMMON

(blank ledger form)

Name_____ Class_____ Date_____

Name _____ Class _____ Date _____

INSTANT REPLAY: SELF-REVIEW QUIZ 18-4

Name _____ Class _____ Date _____

CONCEPT CHECK

1. _____

_____

_____

_____

2.   <u>To Preferred</u>   <u>To Common</u>

_____

_____

_____

_____

_____

3.

CONCEPT CHECK (CONCLUDED)

4. _____

_____

_____

_____

_____

_____

_____

_____

_____

_____

_____

_____

_____

5.

FORMS FOR EXERCISES A or B

18A-1 OR 18B-1

18A-2 OR 18B-2

18A-3 OR 18B-3

Year	Dividend to Preferred Stock	Dividend to Common Stock
1		
2		
3		

EXERCISES (CONCLUDED)

18A-4 OR 18B-4

18A-5 OR 18B-5

END OF CHAPTER PROBLEMS

PROBLEM 18A-1 OR PROBLEM 18B-1

(1)

GRACIE CORPORATION
GENERAL JOURNAL   PAGE 3

Date	Account Titles and Description	PR	Dr.	Cr.

PROBLEM 18A-1 OR PROBLEM 18B-1 (CONTINUED)

(1)

PREFERRED STOCK   ACCOUNT NO. 310

Date	Explanation	Post Ref.	Debit	Credit	Balance Debit	Balance Credit

PAID-IN CAPITAL IN EXCESS OF PAR-PREFERRED   ACCOUNT NO. 311

Date	Explanation	Post Ref.	Debit	Credit	Balance Debit	Balance Credit

COMMON STOCK   ACCOUNT NO. 312

Date	Explanation	Post Ref.	Debit	Credit	Balance Debit	Balance Credit

PAID-IN CAPITAL IN EXCESS OF PAR-COMMON   ACCOUNT NO. 313

Date	Explanation	Post Ref.	Debit	Credit	Balance Debit	Balance Credit

PROBLEM 18A-1 OR PROBLEM 18B-1 (CONCLUDED)

(2)

PROBLEM 18A-2 OR PROBLEM 18B-2

		2011	2012	2013	2014	2015
A)						
B)						
C)						

WORK AREA

PROBLEM 18A-3 OR PROBLEM 18B-3

UNUNOCTIUM CORPORATION
STOCKHOLDER'S EQUITY
JULY 31, 201X

PROBLEM 18A-4 OR PROBLEM 18B-4

PROKO COMPANY
GENERAL JOURNAL

PAGE 6

Date	Account Titles and Description	PR	Dr.	Cr.

PROBLEM 18A-4 OR PROBLEM 18B-4 (CONTINUED)

Common Stock	310

Paid-in Capital in Excess of Par Value-Common	311

Common Stock Subscribed	312

PROBLEM 18A-4 OR PROBLEM 18B-4 (CONCLUDED)

PROKO CORPORATION
STOCKHOLDER'S EQUITY
OCTOBER 31, 201X

CHAPTER 18
SUMMARY PRACTICE TEST:
CORPORATIONS—ORGANIZATIONS AND STOCK

Part I Instructions

Fill in the blank(s) to complete the statement.

1. Market value does not mean _____ _____.

2. _____ _____ _____ are usually drawn up by lawyers when applying to a state for a charter.

3. The board of directors _____ the officers of a corporation.

4. There is no _____ _____ in a corporation compared to a partnership.

5. A(n) _____ _____ _____ requires a corporation to adhere to many federal and state regulations.

6. _____ _____ is not cash.

7. Retained Earnings doesn't mean _____.

8. Often a corporation doesn't issue all the _____ stock.

9. _____ _____ represents the amount of stock in the hands of the stockholders.

10. _____ _____ is the right to maintain one's proportionate interest in the company.

11. Holders of _____ _____ may give up voting rights.

12. _____ _____ is an arbitrary value placed on each share of stock.

13. Stock could be issued with no par value with a(n) _____ _____.

14. Stated value doesn't mean _____ _____.

15. An amount a corporation must retain in the business for protection of the creditors is called _____ _____.

16. Undeclared dividends will accumulate to holders of _____ preferred stock.

17. _____ preferred stock will limit the amount of dividends to preferred stockholders.

18. Paid-in Capital in Excess of Par Value is found on the _____ _____.

19. Organization cost is _____ rather than an asset on the balance sheet.

20. Common Stock Subscribed is a temporary _____ _____ account.

Part II Instructions

Match the term in the column on the left to the definition, example, or phrase in the column on the right. Be sure to use a letter only once.

__h__   **1.** EXAMPLE: Common Stock Subscribed

_____   **2.** Retained Earnings

_____   **3.** Nonparticipating preferred stock

_____   **4.** Par value

_____   **5.** Stated value

_____   **6.** Cumulative

_____   **7.** Paid-in Capital in Excess of Stated Value—Common

_____   **8.** Preemptive right

_____   **9.** Expensed

_____   **10.** Discount on common stock

_____   **11.** No voting rights

_____   **12.** Legal Capital

_____   **13.** Outstanding stock

_____   **14.** Paid-in Capital in Excess of Par Value—Common

_____   **15.** Pay for stock in installments

a. Organization cost

b. Dividends in arrears accumulate

c. Premium from sale of no par common stock with stated value

d. Proportionate ownership

e. Limits amount of dividends to preferred stockholders each year

f. Stock subscriptions

g. A change must be approved by state

h. Temporary stockholders' equity

i. Premium from sale of par value common stock

j. Can change without approval of state

k. Stock in hands of stockholders

l. Accumulated profits that are retained in the corporation

m. Preferred stock

n. Protection of creditors

o. Contra-stockholders' equity account

Part III Instructions

Answer true or false to the following.

1. Subscriptions Receivable—Common Stock is a current asset on the balance sheet.
2. Paid-in Capital in Excess of Par—common represents stock sold at a discount.
3. Common Stock Subscribed is a temporary stockholders' equity account.
4. Organization Costs is an intangible asset.
5. Stock can be exchanged for non cash assets.
6. No par common stock could be sold with a stated value.

7. Discount on Common Stock is a contra-liability account.
8. Preferred stock can only be cumulative.
9. Total par value is used to allocate dividends to participating preferred stock.
10. Nonparticipating preferred stock increases the possible dividends to preferred each year.
11. A cumulative dividend must be paid.
12. Stated value is not allowed in most states.
13. Legal capital helps protect the rights of creditors.
14. Par value is arbitrary.
15. Market value and stated value are the same.
16. Preferred stock is more risky than common stock.
17. Preemptive rights apply only to preferred stock.
18. Issued stock represents the number of authorized shares.
19. Stockholders' equity is composed of paid-in capital and retained earnings.
20. Retained Earnings and Cash accounts will have the same balance.

CHAPTER 18
SOLUTIONS TO SUMMARY PRACTICE TEST

Part I

1. par value
2. Articles of incorporation
3. appoints
4. unlimited liability
5. certificate of incorporation
6. Retained Earnings
7. cash
8. authorized
9. Outstanding stock
10. Preemptive right
11. preferred stock
12. Par value
13. stated value
14. market value
15. legal capital
16. cumulative
17. Nonparticipating
18. balance sheet
19. expensed
20. stockholders' equity

Part II

1.	h	**6.**	b	**11.**	m
2.	l	**7.**	c	**12.**	n
3.	e	**8.**	d	**13.**	k
4.	g	**9.**	a	**14.**	i
5.	j	**10.**	o	**15.**	f

Part III

1.	true	**11.**	false
2.	false	**12.**	false
3.	true	**13.**	true
4.	true	**14.**	true
5.	true	**15.**	false
6.	true	**16.**	false
7.	false	**17.**	false
8.	false	**18.**	false
9.	true	**19.**	true
10.	false	**20.**	false

CORPORATIONS: STOCK VALUES, DIVIDENDS, TREASURY STOCKS, AND RETAINED EARNINGS

19

INSTANT REPLAY: SELF-REVIEW QUIZ 19-1

INSTANT REPLAY: SELF-REVIEW QUIZ 19-2

INSTANT REPLAY: SELF-REVIEW QUIZ 19-3

Name _____ Class _____ Date _____

INSTANT REPLAY: SELF-REVIEW QUIZ 19-4

CONCEPT CHECK

1.

2.

3.

4.

5.

FORMS FOR EXERCISES A or B

19A-1 OR 19B-1

_____

_____

_____

_____

_____

19A-2 OR 19B-2

Date		Account Titles and Description	PR		Dr.			Cr.	

19A-3 OR 19B-3

Date		Account Titles and Description	PR		Dr.			Cr.	

EXERCISES (CONCLUDED)

19A-4 OR 19B-4

Date		Account Titles and Description	PR		Dr.		Cr.	

_____

_____

_____

_____

_____

19A-5 OR 19B-5

DONALD COMPANY
STATEMENT OF RETAINED EARNINGS
YEAR ENDED DECEMBER 31, 20X4

END OF CHAPTER PROBLEMS

PROBLEM 19A-1 OR PROBLEM 19B-1

Name _____ Class _____ Date _____

PROBLEM 19A-2 OR PROBLEM 19B-2

RACE CORPORATION
GENERAL JOURNAL

PAGE 4

Date		Account Titles and Description	PR		Dr.		Cr.

PROBLEM 19A-3 OR PROBLEM 19B-3

MOUNTAIN VIEW CORPORATION
GENERAL JOURNAL

PAGE 3

Date	Account Titles and Description	PR	Dr.	Cr.

PROBLEM 19A-3 OR PROBLEM 19B-3 (CONTINUED)

COMMON STOCK   ACCOUNT NO. 312

Date	Explanation	Post Ref.	Debit	Credit	Balance Debit	Balance Credit

COMMON STOCK DIVIDEND DISTRIBUTABLE   ACCOUNT NO. 313

Date	Explanation	Post Ref.	Debit	Credit	Balance Debit	Balance Credit

PAID-IN CAPITAL IN EXCESS OF PAR VALUE—COMMON   ACCOUNT NO. 314

Date	Explanation	Post Ref.	Debit	Credit	Balance Debit	Balance Credit

PAID-IN CAPITAL IN EXCESS OF PAR VALUE—STOCK DIVIDEND   ACCOUNT NO. 315

Date	Explanation	Post Ref.	Debit	Credit	Balance Debit	Balance Credit

TREASURY STOCK   ACCOUNT NO. 316

Date	Explanation	Post Ref.	Debit	Credit	Balance Debit	Balance Credit

Name _____ Class _____ Date _____

PROBLEM 19A-3 OR PROBLEM 19B-3 (CONTINUED)

PAID-IN CAPITAL FROM TREASURY STOCK   ACCOUNT NO. <u>317</u>

Date	Explanation	Post Ref.	Debit	Credit	Balance Debit	Balance Credit

RETAINED EARNINGS   ACCOUNT NO. <u>319</u>

Date	Explanation	Post Ref.	Debit	Credit	Balance Debit	Balance Credit

PROBLEM 19A-3 OR PROBLEM 19B-3 (CONTINUED)

MOUNTAIN VIEW CORPORATION
STOCKHOLDERS' EQUITY

PROBLEM 19A-3 OR PROBLEM 19B-3 (CONCLUDED)

MOUNTAIN VIEW CORPORATION
STATEMENT OF RETAINED EARNINGS
YEAR ENDED DECEMBER 201X

Name _____ Class _____ Date _____

PROBLEM 19A-4 OR PROBLEM 19B-4

PIESCO CORPORATION
GENERAL JOURNAL   PAGE 12

Date		Account Titles and Description	PR		Dr.			Cr.		

PROBLEM 19A-4 OR PROBLEM 19B-4 (CONTINUED)

PREFERRED STOCK   ACCOUNT NO. 310

Date	Explanation	Post Ref.	Debit	Credit	Balance Debit	Balance Credit

PAID-IN CAPITAL IN EXCESS OF PAR VALUE—PREFERRED   ACCOUNT NO. 311

Date	Explanation	Post Ref.	Debit	Credit	Balance Debit	Balance Credit

COMMON STOCK   ACCOUNT NO. 314

Date	Explanation	Post Ref.	Debit	Credit	Balance Debit	Balance Credit

COMMON STOCK DIVIDEND DISTRIBUTABLE   ACCOUNT NO. 315

Date	Explanation	Post Ref.	Debit	Credit	Balance Debit	Balance Credit

PAID-IN CAPITAL IN EXCESS OF PAR—COMMON   ACCOUNT NO. 316

Date	Explanation	Post Ref.	Debit	Credit	Balance Debit	Balance Credit

PROBLEM 19A-4 OR PROBLEM 19B-4 (CONTINUED)

PAID-IN CAPITAL IN EXCESS OF PAR VALUE—STOCK DIVIDEND   ACCOUNT NO. 318

Date	Explanation	Post Ref.	Debit	Credit	Balance Debit	Balance Credit

TREASURY STOCK   ACCOUNT NO. 320

Date	Explanation	Post Ref.	Debit	Credit	Balance Debit	Balance Credit

PAID-IN CAPITAL FROM TREASURY STOCK   ACCOUNT NO. 321

Date	Explanation	Post Ref.	Debit	Credit	Balance Debit	Balance Credit

RETAINED EARNINGS   ACCOUNT NO. 330

Date	Explanation	Post Ref.	Debit	Credit	Balance Debit	Balance Credit

PROBLEM 19A-4 OR PROBLEM 19B-4 (CONCLUDED)

(2)

PIESCO CORPORATION
STOCKHOLDERS' EQUITY

CHAPTER 19
SUMMARY PRACTICE TEST:
CORPORATIONS: STOCK VALUES,
DIVIDENDS, TREASURY STOCKS, AND
RETAINED EARNINGS

Part I Instructions

Fill in the blank(s) to complete the statement.

1. _____ _____ is the price that a corporation pays to retire or redeem stock.

2. _____ _____, which is often used by companies for comparative and analytical purposes, is based on cost and not current market price.

3. A distribution of earnings could result in a(n) _____.

4. The _____ _____ _____ will establish which stockholders will receive the dividend.

5. To pay a dividend, there must be a sufficient balance in cash and _____ _____.

6. Dividends Payable is a(n) _____ _____ on the balance sheet.

7. On the date of record, _____ _____ is made.

8. The issuance of unissued stock to stockholders instead of a distribution of assets is the result of a(n) _____ _____.

9. A stock dividend will not reduce total _____ _____ the way a cash dividend will.

10. The _____ _____ of Common Stock Dividend Distributable is a credit.

11. The _____ _____ of a corporation remains the same as before and after a stock dividend.

12. A(n) _____ _____ doesn't change the Retained Earnings account the way a stock dividend does.

13. Previously issued preferred or common stock that has been reacquired by the corporation is known as _____ _____.

14. Treasury stock is recognized as _____ but not _____ for voting or dividend purposes.

15. Treasury stock is a(n) _____ stockholders' equity account.

Name _____ Class _____ Date _____

Part II Instructions

Match the term in the column on the left to the definition, example, or phrase in the column on the right. Be sure to use a letter only once.

__j__   **1.** EXAMPLE: Appropriation of retained earnings

_____   **2.** A contra stockholders' equity account

_____   **3.** Date of record

_____   **4.** Cash dividend

_____   **5.** Stock dividend

_____   **6.** Normal balance of treasury stock

_____   **7.** Normal balance of common stock

_____   **8.** Statement of retained earnings

_____   **9.** Book value

_____ **10.** Not outstanding

_____ **11.** Paid-in capital from treasury stock

_____ **12.** Stock split

_____ **13.** Date of declaration

_____ **14.** Market value

a.   Determined in open market

b.   Category of treasury stock

c.   Distribution of earnings in the form of cash

d.   Determines who receives dividend

e.   Never a negative balance

f.   Previously unissued stock is issued

g.   Disposing of assets without any losses

h.   Debit

i.   Treasury stock

j.   Restrict amount of retained earnings available for dividend

k.   Credit

l.   Use for stock option plan

m.   Dividend Payable created

n.   Formal report

o.   Doesn't change Retained Earnings

Part III Instructions

Answer true or false to the following.

1. Dividends are subtracted from beginning retained earnings in the statement of retained earnings.
2. If net income was overstated in a prior period, Retained Earnings of the prior period was also overstated.
3. A statement of retained earnings is an informal report.
4. Appropriations of retained earnings results from involuntary reasons.
5. Treasury stock does not change the amount of issued stock.
6. Treasury stock reduces the number of shares outstanding.
7. Treasury stock is subtracted from stockholders' equity.
8. A decrease in the Treasury Stock account will result in an increase to stockholders' equity.
9. Treasury stock is recorded at par value.
10. Treasury stock is really a liability.

11. Treasury stock could never be received in the settlement of a debt.
12. A stock split will increase the number of shares outstanding.
13. Book value and market value are really the same for most corporations.
14. A stock dividend will result in total stockholders' equity increasing.
15. Common Stock Dividend Distributable is an asset.
16. Common Stock Dividend Distributable is only recorded at the market price.
17. A stock dividend does require some cash.
18. Stock dividends do increase permanent capital in the business.
19. Dividends payable is recorded only at the date of record.
20. Redemption value ignores all dividends in arrears.

CHAPTER 19
SOLUTIONS TO SUMMARY PRACTICE TEST

Part I

1. Redemption value
2. Book value
3. dividend
4. date of record
5. retained earnings
6. current liability
7. no entry
8. stock dividend
9. stockholders' equity
10. normal balance
11. book value
12. stock split
13. treasury stock
14. issued, outstanding
15. contra

Part II

1. j
2. b
3. d
4. c
5. f
6. h
7. k
8. n
9. g
10. i
11. e
12. o
13. m
14. a

Part III

1. true
2. true
3. false
4. false
5. true
6. true
7. true
8. true
9. false
10. false
11. false
12. true
13. false
14. false
15. false
16. false
17. false
18. true
19. false
20. false

CORPORATIONS AND BONDS PAYABLE

20

INSTANT REPLAY: SELF-REVIEW QUIZ 20-1

Name _____ Class _____ Date _____

INSTANT REPLAY: SELF-REVIEW QUIZ 20-2

PERIOD	CARRYING VALUE, BEG. OF PERIOD	TOTAL INTEREST EXPENSE	INTEREST PAID TO BONDHOLDERS	AMORTIZED DISCOUNT TRANSF. TO INCREASE INTEREST EXPENSE	(BOOK VALUE) CARRYING VALUE, END OF PERIOD
1					
2					
3					

INSTANT REPLAY: SELF-REVIEW QUIZ 20-3

PERIOD	(1) CARRYING AMOUNT, BEG. OF PERIOD	(2) INTEREST PAID TO BONDHOLDERS (.06 x FACE VALUE)	(3) INTEREST EXPENSE TO BE RECORDED (.07 x CARRYING VALUE)	(4) DISCOUNT TO BE AMORTIZED	(5) CARRYING AMOUNT, END OF PERIOD
1					
2					
3					

Name _____ Class _____ Date _____

INSTANT REPLAY: SELF-REVIEW QUIZ 20-4

(blank accounting worksheet grid)

CONCEPT CHECK

1.

A.

B.

C.

2.

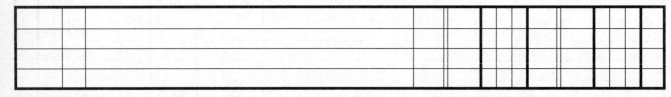

3.

4.

5.

CONCEPT CHECK (CONCLUDED)

6. A. _____
    _____
    _____
    _____

    B. _____
    C. _____
    D. _____
    E. _____

7.

8. A. _____
    B. _____
    C. _____
    D. _____
    E. _____

9.

10.

FORMS FOR EXERCISES A or B

20A-1 OR 20B-1

	Boice	Hopkins
Earnings before Taxes or Finance Cost		
Less: Bond Interest		
Earnings Subject to Income Tax		
Less: Income Tax (30%)		
Net Income		
Less: Preferred Dividend		
Earnings for Common Stockholders		
Number of Common Stock Shares Outstanding		
Earnings per Share		

20A-2 OR 20B-2

EXERCISES (CONTINUED)

20A-3 OR 20B-3

20A-4 OR 20B-4

Name _____ Class _____ Date _____

EXERCISES (CONCLUDED)

20A-5 OR 20B-5

20A-6 OR 20B-6

20A-7 OR 20B-7 _____

_____

_____

_____

_____

_____

_____

_____

END OF CHAPTER PROBLEMS

PROBLEM 20A-1 OR PROBLEM 20B-1

LEMMING CORPORATION
AMORTIZATION SCHEDULE

PERIOD	CARRYING VALUE BEG. OF PERIOD	TOTAL INTEREST EXPENSE	INTEREST TO BONDHOLDERS (RATE x FACE)	AMORTIZED DISCOUNT TO INCREASE INT. EXP.	UNAMORTIZED DISCOUNT END OF PERIOD	CARRYING VALUE END OF PERIOD

(2)

PROBLEM 20A-1 OR PROBLEM 20B-1 (CONCLUDED)

PROBLEM 20A-2 OR PROBLEM 20B-2

LESTER CORPORATION
AMORTIZATION SCHEDULE

PERIOD	CARRYING VALUE	TOTAL INTEREST EXPENSE	INTEREST TO BE PAID BONDHOLDERS (RATE x FACE)	AMORTIZED PREMIUM TO DECREASE INTEREST EXP.	UNAMORTIZED PREMIUM AT END OF PERIOD	CARRYING VALUE AT END OF PERIOD

Name _____ Class _____ Date _____

PROBLEM 20A-3 OR PROBLEM 20B-3

ACORN CORPORATION
AMORTIZATION SCHEDULE

(1)

PERIOD	CARRYING AMOUNT BEG. OF PERIOD	INTEREST PAID TO BONDHOLDERS	INTEREST EXPENSE TO BE RECORDED	DISCOUNT TO BE AMORTIZED	UNAMORTIZED DISCOUNT	CARRYING VALUE END OF PERIOD

(2)

(3)

PROBLEM 20A-4 OR PROBLEM 20B-4

LEFLER CORPORATION
AMORTIZATION SCHEDULE

(1)

PERIOD	CARRYING VALUE BEG. OF PERIOD	INTEREST PAID TO BONDHOLDERS	INTEREST EXPENSE TO BE RECORDED	PREMIUM TO BE AMORTIZED	UNAMORTIZED PREMIUM	VALUE END OF PERIOD

(2)

Name _____ Class _____ Date _____

CHAPTER 20
SUMMARY PRACTICE TEST:
CORPORATIONS AND BONDS PAYABLE

Part I Instructions

Fill in the blank(s) to complete the statement.

1. _____ are not the same as stock.

2. The _____ _____ is the annual interest rate, which is based on face value.

3. Usually bond agreements are monitored by a(n) _____ to represent the group of bondholders.

4. A $1,000 bond with a quote of 88 means it is currently selling for _____.

5. _____ _____ are bonds in which the corporation pledges no specific assets as collateral.

6. Bond _____ is deductible from earnings before tax.

7. _____ are deducted after tax on earnings.

8. Most bondholders receive interest _____.

9. _____ _____ could mean that the buyer of a bond pays more than the purchase price.

10. A bond whose contract rate is less than the market rate is probably selling at a(n) _____.

11. A bond discount is a(n) _____ _____ account.

12. The _____ _____ of a bond is the cost of the bond to be paid back at maturity less the discount or plus the premium.

13. The _____ of a bond discount will increase the total interest expense for that period.

14. If the contract rate of a bond is greater than the market rate of a bond, it is probably selling at a(n) _____.

15. The amortization of a bond premium will _____ the total interest expense for that period.

16. The _____ _____ means that the amortization of discounts or premiums is a constant percentage of the bond's carrying value.

17. A(n) _____ _____ will accumulate assets over the life of the bond to pay off the bondholders at maturity.

Part II Instructions

Match the term in the column on the left with the definition, example, or phrase in the column on the right. Be sure to use a letter only once.

__i__   **1.**   EXAMPLE: Sinking Fund Earned

_____   **2.**   Secured bond

_____   **3.**   Interest method of amortization

_____   **4.**   Bond interest

_____   **5.** $1,000 denominations

_____   **6.**   Discount on Bonds Payable

_____   **7.**   Contract interest rate

_____   **8.**   Carrying value

_____   **9.**   Straight-line method of amortization

_____   **10.**   Dividend

_____   **11.**   Premium on Bonds Payable

_____   **12.**   Registered bond

_____   **13.**   Effective rate

_____   **14.**   Coupon bond

_____   **15.**   Sinking fund

a.   Fund used to pay off bonds at maturity

b.   Real or actual rate of interest

c.   Owners of bonds are not registered

d.   Amount of premium or discount amortized is the same for each period

e.   Stated rate of interest

f.   Contra-liability account

g.   Carrying value of bond times market rate

h.   Bonds

i.   Other revenue account

j.   Corporation's assets used to secure bonds

k.   Face value and bond premium

l.   Distribution of net income after tax

m.   Bond interest sent directly to bondholder

n.   Deductible expense before tax

o.   Bonds issued above face value

Part III Instructions

Answer true or false to the following.

1.   Bond refunding results in a lower rate of interest.

2.   A bond being retired before the maturity date must have any amortization of discount or premium brought up to date.

3.   Bond Sinking Fund is a liability.

4.   Sinking Fund Earned is an asset.

5.   Discount on Bonds Payable may require an adjusting year-end entry.

6.   Interest expense to bondholders is the face value divided by the contract rate.

7.   Under the interest method of amortizing the bond discount, interest expense in each period will not be the same amount.

8.   Accountants prefer the amortization of bond discounts and premiums by straight-line method over the interest method.

9.   Premium on Bonds Payable is a contra-liability.

10.   Amortization of a bond premium will reduce interest expense for that period.

11.   When amortized, Discount on Bonds Payable will increase total Bond Interest expense.

12.   Six percent is the semiannual rate of 12 percent per annum.

13.   Bond discounts can only be amortized by the straight-line method.

14. Face value plus premium equals new carrying value.
15. Face value less bond discount equals old carrying value.
16. Discount on Bonds Payable is a contra asset.
17. A company's estimated year interest rate is called the effective rate.
18. Purchasers of bonds may have to pay accrued interest.
19. Bondholders have no voting rights.
20. Interest Expense on bonds is a fixed charge to a company.

CHAPTER 20

SOLUTIONS TO PRACTICE SUMMARY TEST

Part I

1. Bonds
2. contract rate
3. trustee
4. $880
5. Debenture bonds
6. interest
7. Dividends
8. semiannually
9. Accrued interest
10. discount
11. contra-liability
12. carrying value
13. amortization
14. premium
15. decrease
16. interest method
17. sinking fund

Part II

1. i
2. j
3. g
4. n
5. h
6. f
7. e
8. k
9. d
10. l
11. o
12. m
13. b
14. c
15. a

Part III

1.	true	**11.**	true
2.	true	**12.**	true
3.	false	**13.**	false
4.	false	**14.**	true
5.	true	**15.**	false
6.	false	**16.**	false
7.	true	**17.**	false
8.	false	**18.**	true
9.	true	**19.**	true
10.	true	**20.**	true

STATEMENT OF CASH FLOWS

21

Name _____ Class _____ Date _____

INSTANT REPLAY: SELF-REVIEW QUIZ 21-1

Name _____ Class _____ Date _____

INSTANT REPLAY: SELF-REVIEW QUIZ 21-2

Name _____ Class _____ Date _____

CONCEPT CHECK

1. A. _____ B. _____ C. _____ D. _____

2.

3.

4.

5.

Name _____ Class _____ Date _____

FORMS FOR EXERCISES A OR B

21A-1 OR 21B-1
_____

_____

21A-2 OR 21B-2

21A-3 OR 21B-3

21A-4 OR 21B-4

A. _____   E. _____

B. _____   F. _____

C. _____

D. _____

END OF CHAPTER PROBLEMS

PROBLEM 21A-1 OR PROBLEM 21B-1

COMPANY
STATEMENT OF CASH FLOWS—INDIRECT METHOD
FOR YEAR ENDED DECEMBER 31, 2012

PROBLEM 21A-2 OR PROBLEM 21B-2

COMPANY
STATEMENT OF CASH FLOWS
FOR YEAR ENDED DECEMBER 31, 2012

CHAPTER 21
SUMMARY PRACTICE TEST:
STATEMENT OF CASH FLOWS

Part I Instructions

Fill in the blank(s) to complete the statement.

1. A business could fail due to a(n) _____ _____ _____.

2. To convert to a cash basis an increase in a current asset will be _____ from net income.

3. _____ _____ _____ _____ _____ includes payment of dividends.

4. _____ _____ reduce Retained Earnings.

5. If accounts receivable is increasing, _____ _____ are increasing more than collections.

6. Sale or purchase of land is part of _____ _____ _____ _____ _____.

7. When using the indirect method, Depreciation expense is _____ to Net Income from operations.

8. In the _____ method we list separate totals for specific operating cash inflows and outflows.

9. Sale of Equipment is a(n) _____ activity.

10. The statement of cash flows can be prepared by the _____ or _____ method.

Part II Instructions

Match the term in the column on the left to the definition, example, or phrase in the column on the right. Be sure to use a letter only once.

__e__ 1. Example: Issue Common Stock   a. Investors are concerned

_____ 2. Positive Cash Flow   b. Mortgage Payable

_____ 3. Has three main parts   c. Lists major groups of cash inflows and outflows for operating activities

_____ 4. Cash Dividends Paid   d. Combine changes in current assets and current liabilities with net income

_____ 5. Purchase or sale of equipment   e. Cash Inflow—Financing Activities

_____ 6. Long-term liability   f. Statement of Cash Flows

_____ 7. Depreciation expense   g. Investing Activities

_____ 8. Indirect Method   h. A non-cash expense

_____ 9. Direct Method   i. Cash Outflow—Financing Activities

Part III Instructions

Answer true or false to the following.

1. The statement of cash flows is a major financial statement.

2. Businesses do not need a positive cash flow to survive.

3. When using the indirect method, net income is added in the section entitled net cash flows from operating activities.

4. When using the indirect method, depreciation is subtracted from net income.

5. When using the indirect method, a decrease in inventory is added to net income.

6. When using the indirect method, an increase in accounts receivable is subtracted from net income.

7. When using the indirect method, an increase in accounts payable is subtracted from net income.

8. Cash flows from investing activities is the name of one section of the statement of cash flows.

9. Current assets are analyzed to calculate cash flows from investing activities.

10. Sale of land is a financing activity.

11. Payment of dividends is a financing activity.

12. When using the direct method, depreciation is added to sales.

13. When using the direct method, a decrease in salaries payable would be added to salary expense.

14. When using the direct method, an increase in inventory is subtracted from sales.

15. When using the direct method, an increase in prepaid insurance is subtracted from insurance expense.

CHAPTER 21
SOLUTIONS TO SUMMARY PRACTICE TEST

Part I

1. negative cash flow

2. subtracted

3. Cash flows from financing activities

4. Cash dividends

5. credit sales

6. Cash flows from investing activities

7. Added

8. Direct

9. Investing

10. direct, indirect

Part II

1. e

2. a

3. f

4. i

5. g

6. b

7. h

8. c

9. d

Part III

1. true

2. false

3. true

4. false

5. true

6. true

7. false

8. true

9. false

10. false

11. true

12. false

13. false

14. true

15. false

ANALYZING FINANCIAL STATEMENTS

INSTANT REPLAY: SELF-REVIEW QUIZ 22-1

	December 31 2013	2012	Amount of Increase or Decrease During 2013	Percent of Increase or Decrease During 2013
Assets				
Current Assets:				
Cash	$ 5,000	$ 4,000		
Accounts Receivable, Net	4,000	2,500		
Merchandise Inventory	6,000	5,600		
Prepaid Expenses	2,000	400		
Total Current Assets				
Plant and Equipment:				
Store Equipment, Net	$146,000	$125,000		
Total Assets				

INSTANT REPLAY: SELF-REVIEW QUIZ 22-2

	2015	2014	2013	2012
Sales				
Cost of Goods Sold				
Gross Profit				

INSTANT REPLAY: SELF-REVIEW QUIZ 22-3

1. Current Ratio $= \dfrac{\text{Current Assets}}{\text{Current Liabilities}} =$

2. Acid-Test $= \dfrac{\text{Current Assets} - \text{Merchandise Inv} - \text{Prepaid Expenses}}{\text{Current Liabilities}} =$

3. Accounts Receivable Turnover $= \dfrac{\text{Net Credit Sales}}{\text{Average Accounts Receivable}} =$

4. Average Collection $= \dfrac{365 \text{ Days}}{\text{Accounts Receivable Turnover}} =$

5. Inventory Turnover $= \dfrac{\text{Cost of Goods Sold}}{\text{Average Inventory}} =$

6. Asset Turnover $= \dfrac{\text{Net Sales}}{\text{Total Assets}} =$

7. Debt to Total Assets $= \dfrac{\text{Total Liabilities}}{\text{Total Assets}} =$

8. Debt to Stockholders' Equity $= \dfrac{\text{Total Liabilities}}{\text{Stockholders' Equity}} =$

9. Times Interest Earned $= \dfrac{\text{Income before Taxes and Interest Expense}}{\text{Interest Expense}} =$

10. Gross Profit Rate $= \dfrac{\text{Gross Profit}}{\text{Net Sales}} =$

11. Return on Sales $= \dfrac{\text{Net Income Before Taxes}}{\text{Net Sales}} =$

12. Rate of Return on Total Assets $= \dfrac{\text{Net Income Before Interest and Taxes}}{\text{Total Assets}} =$

13. Rate of Return on $= \dfrac{\text{Net Income Before Taxes} - \text{Preferred Dividends}}{\text{Common Stockholders' Equity}} =$

CONCEPT CHECK

1.   A.   B.

2.   A.   B.

                     C.   D.

3.

4.

5.   A.   B.

                     C.   D.

FORMS FOR EXERCISES A OR B

22A-1 OR 22A-2

ASHER COMPANY
INCOME STATEMENT
FOR THE YEAR ENDED DEC. 31 20X9 AND 20X8

	DECEMBER 31		AMOUNT OF INCREASE OR DECREASE DURING 2013	PERCENT OF INCREASE OR DECREASE DURING 2013
	2013	2012		

22A-2 OR 22B-2

TONY CO.
COMMON-SIZE COMPARATIVE INCOME STATEMENT
FOR YEARS ENDED DECEMBER 31, 2013 AND 2012

	2013	2012

EXERCISES (CONCLUDED)

22A-3 OR 22B-3

HOWE COMPANY
COMMON-SIZE COMPARATIVE BALANCE SHEET
DECEMBER 31, 2013 AND 2012

	2013	2012

22A-4 OR 22B-4

	2015	2014	2013	2012
Sales				
Gross Profit				
Net Income				

22A-5 OR 22B-5

A. _____   B. _____   C. _____

_____   _____   _____

_____   _____   _____

_____   _____   _____

_____   _____   _____

_____   _____   _____

_____   _____   _____

END OF CHAPTER PROBLEMS

PROBLEM 22A-1 OR PROBLEM 22B-1

(A)

DEAN CORPORATION
COMPARATIVE BALANCE SHEET
DEC. 31, 2013 AND 2012

	2013	2012	AMOUNT OF INCREASE OR DECREASE DURING 2013	PERCENT OF INCREASE OR DECREASE DURING 2013

PROBLEM 22A-1 OR PROBLEM 22B-1 (CONCLUDED)

DEAN CORPORATION
BALANCE SHEET
DECEMBER 31, 2013

(B)

		2013		%

PROBLEM 22A-2 OR PROBLEM 22B-2

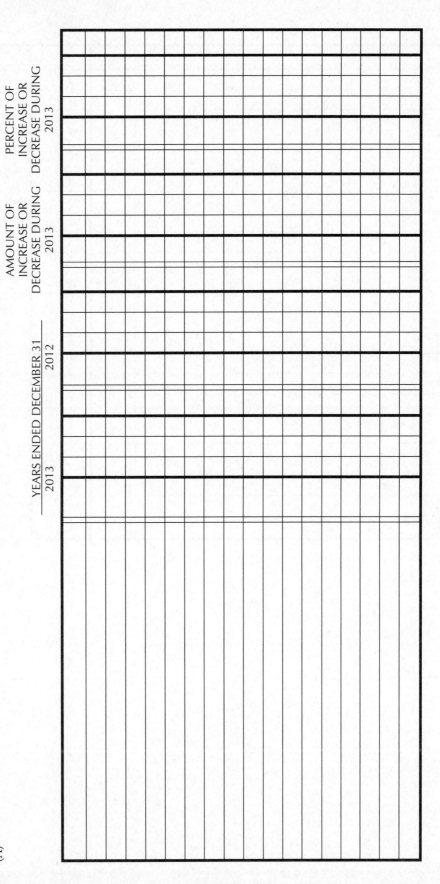

(A)

PROBLEM 22A-2 OR PROBLEM 22B-2 (CONTINUED)

(B)   2013   %

PROBLEM 22A-2 OR PROBLEM 22B-2 (CONCLUDED)

(C)   2013   2012

PROBLEM 22A-3 OR PROBLEM 22B-3

PROBLEM 22A-3 OR PROBLEM 22B-3 (CONCLUDED)

PROBLEM 22A-4 OR PROBLEM 22B-4

(A)

Name_____ Class_____ Date_____

PROBLEM 22A-4 OR PROBLEM 22B-4 (CONTINUED)

VALE CORPORATION
COMMON-SIZE COMPARATIVE INCOME STATEMENT
FOR YEARS ENDED DECEMBER 31, 2013, 2012, 2011

(B)

		2013	2012	2011

PROBLEM 22A-4 OR PROBLEM 22B-4 (CONCLUDED)

(C)   2013   2012   2011

CHAPTER 22

SUMMARY PRACTICE TEST:
ANALYZING FINANCIAL STATEMENTS

Part I Instructions

Fill in the blank(s) to complete the statement.

1. _____ _____ could be helpful in ratio analysis.

2. _____ analysis uses a base year to calculate the percentage change of each item.

3. _____ _____ computes the amount of increase or decrease of each account on the comparative balance sheet along with each percentage change.

4. _____ from horizontal analysis cannot be totalled vertically.

5. Horizontal analysis on the income statement calculates amounts and rates of change between _____ _____ of time.

6. Balance sheet horizontal analysis calculates amounts and rates of change between _____ _____ of time.

7. A(n) _____ _____ comparative income statement is expressed in percents without dollar amounts.

8. Trend analysis is a type of _____ _____.

9. A(n) _____ is the relationship of one amount to another that results by dividing one by the other.

10. _____ ratios help companies measure their ability to meet short-term obligations.

11. _____ _____ ratios help companies measure how well they are utilizing their assets.

12. _____ _____ ratios help companies analyze their mixture of debt and equity mix.

13. _____ ratios measure a company's ability to earn profit.

Name _____ Class _____ Date _____

Part II Instructions

Match the term in the column on the left to the definition, example, or phrase in the column on the right. Be sure to use a letter only once.

_____c_____ 1. EXAMPLE: Current ratio   a. Accounts receivable turnover
_____ 2. Asset turnover   b. Gross profits divided by net sales
_____ 3. Trend analysis   c. Current assets divided by current liabilities
_____ 4. Ratio   d. Relationship of one amount to another
_____ 5. Gross profit rate   e. Less cash tied up in inventory
_____ 6. Quick assets   f. Reveals amount of assets financed by the creditors
_____ 7. Degree of risk to creditors g. Debt versus equity
_____ 8. Comparative financial reports h. Times interest earned
_____ 9. How many times accounts   i. No dollar amounts
             receivable turned into cash j. Net sales divided by total assets
_____ 10. Debt to total assets   k. Two or more successive periods analyzed
_____ 11. Debt management ratio   l. Current assets less merch. inv. less prep. exp.
_____ 12. Inventory   m. Uses a base year
_____ 13. Return on sales   n. Not easily converted into cash
_____ 14. Common size   o. Net income before taxes divided by net sales
_____ 15. High inventory turnover

Part III Instructions

Answer true or false to the following.

1. Financial ratios are never compared to industrial averages.
2. Creditors are the only ones concerned with analyzing financial reports.
3. Horizontal analysis cannot be done on comparative balance sheets.
4. Percentages from horizontal analysis can be totaled vertically.
5. Vertical analysis cannot be done on balance sheets.
6. Common-size statements do not use dollar amounts.
7. Prepaid expenses are easily converted into cash.
8. A base year is chosen when trend analysis is done.
9. A ratio is the relationship of one amount to another that results by multiplying one by the other.
10. Liquidity ratios measure a company's ability to earn profit.
11. How well a company is using its assets is measured by asset-management ratios.
12. The acid-test ratio is calculated by current assets divided by long-term liabilities.
13. The higher accounts receivable turnover is, the slower the accounts receivable is turning into cash.

14. Inventory turnover amounts will vary from industry to industry.

15. Profitability ratios measure a company's ability to earn profits.

16. The asset turnover shows the amount of assets financed by creditors.

17. Degree of risk to creditors if a company defaults on interest payments is shown in the times-interest-earned ratio.

18. The gross profit turnover shows how much a company earns on each sales dollar.

19. Rate of return on common stockholders' equity measures the ability of a company to look at how a company's assets are financed.

20. A low inventory turnover could possibly mean excessive investment in assets.

CHAPTER 22
SOLUTIONS TO SUMMARY PRACTICE TEST

Part I

1. Industry averages
2. Trend
3. Horizontal analysis
4. Percentages
5. two periods
6. two points
7. common-size
8. horizontal analysis
9. ratio
10. Liquidity
11. Asset management
12. Debt management
13. Profitability

Part II

1. c
2. j
3. m
4. d
5. b
6. l
7. h
8. k
9. a
10. f
11. g
12. n
13. o
14. i
15. e

Part III

1.	false	**11.**	true
2.	false	**12.**	false
3.	false	**13.**	false
4.	false	**14.**	true
5.	false	**15.**	true
6.	true	**16.**	false
7.	false	**17.**	true
8.	true	**18.**	false
9.	false	**19.**	false
10.	false	**20.**	true

23

THE VOUCHER SYSTEM

INSTANT REPLAY: SELF-REVIEW QUIZ 23-1

1. _____ 2. _____ 3. _____ 4. _____ 5. _____

INSTANT REPLAY: SELF-REVIEW QUIZ 23-2

VOUCHER REGISTER

Date	Voucher Number	Payable to	Date of Payment	Check No.	Voucher Payable Cr.	Purchases Dr.	Account	PR	Dr.	Cr.

Sundry Accounts

CONCEPT CHECK

1.

2.

3.

4.

5A.

5B.

Name _____ Class _____ Date _____

FORMS FOR EXERCISES A OR B

23A-1 OR 23B-1

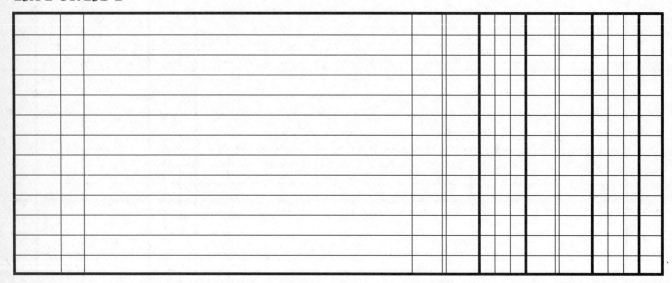

23A-2 OR 23B-2

23A-3 OR 23B-3

EXERCISES (CONCLUDED)

23A-4 OR 23B-4

23A-5 OR 23B-5
(A)

(B)

END OF CHAPTER PROBLEMS

PROBLEM 23A-1 OR PROBLEM 23B-1

FAERAH CORPORATION
VOUCHER REGISTER

PAGE 8

Date	Voucher Number	Payable to	Date of Payment	Check No.	Voucher Payable Cr.	Purchases Dr.	Account	PR	Sundry Accounts Dr.	Sundry Accounts Cr.

PROBLEM 23A-2 OR PROBLEM 23B-2

PAGE 9

VOUCHER REGISTER

Date	Voucher Number	Payable to	Date of Payment	Check No.	Voucher Payable Cr.	Purchases Dr.	Account	PR	Sundry Accounts Dr.	Cr.

PROBLEM 23A-2 OR PROBLEM 23B-2 (CONCLUDED)

CHECK REGISTER

PAGE 7

Date	Check No.	Payable to	Voucher No.	Voucher Payable Dr.			Purchases Discount Cr.			Cash Cr.		

PROBLEM 23A-3 OR PROBLEM 23B-3

VOUCHER REGISTER

PAGE 9

Date	Voucher Number	Payable to	Date of Payment	Check No.	Voucher Payable Cr.	Purchases Dr.	Sundry Accounts			
							Account	PR	Dr.	Cr.

Name _____ Class _____ Date _____

PROBLEM 23A-3 OR PROBLEM 23B-3 (CONCLUDED)

CHECK REGISTER   PAGE 4

Date	Check No.	Payable to	Voucher No.	Voucher Payable Dr.	Purchases Discount Cr.	Cash Cr.

PROBLEM 23A-4 OR PROBLEM 23B-4

VOUCHER REGISTER

PAGE 9

Date	Voucher Number	Payable to	Date of Payment	Check No.	Voucher Payable Cr.	Purchases Dr.	Account	PR	Sundry Accounts Dr.	Sundry Accounts Cr.

PROBLEM 23A-4 OR PROBLEM 23B-4 (CONCLUDED)

CHECK REGISTER   PAGE 8

Date	Check No.	Payable to	Voucher No.	Voucher Payable Dr.	Purchases Discount Cr.	Cash Cr.

CHAPTER 23
SUMMARY PRACTICE TEST:
THE VOUCHER SYSTEM

Part I Instructions

Fill in the blank(s) to complete the statement.

1. Large corporations may use a(n) _____ _____.

2. Supporting documents are attached to the front of the _____.

3. An invoice is usually compared to the purchase requisition and _____ _____.

4. The account distribution on the back of the voucher is approved by the _____ _____.

5. Vouchers are entered into the voucher register in _____ _____ at the time the liability is incurred.

6. The _____ _____ _____ contains each unpaid voucher by the due date.

7. The _____ _____ account replaces the title Accounts Payable in the voucher and check register.

8. The _____ _____ in a voucher system replaces the cash payments journal.

9. In the check register, the check numbers are listed in _____ _____.

10. A(n) _____ _____ _____ _____ can be prepared from the unpaid voucher file at the end of the month.

11. _____ _____ is a title that would be used to show any discounts lost assuming invoices were recorded at net.

12. If a net approach is used to record invoices, there is no need for the _____ _____ account.

13. For partial payments after a voucher has been prepared, the older voucher is _____ and a new voucher is prepared for each installment.

14. Vouchers Payable have a(n) _____ balance.

15. In a voucher system, the _____ _____ _____ is eliminated.

Part II Instructions

Match the term in the column on the left to the definition, example, or phrase in the column on the right. Be sure to use a letter only once.

__f__   **1.** EXAMPLE: Discount lost
_____   **2.** A source document
_____   **3.** Voucher defaced
_____   **4.** Controls cash payments
_____   **5.** Account distribution
_____   **6.** Schedule of vouchers payable
_____   **7.** Normal balance of Vouchers Payable
_____   **8.** Cancelling original voucher
_____   **9.** Listed in check number sequence
_____   **10.** Partial payments
_____   **11.** Retention of paid vouchers
_____   **12.** Vouchers filed by due date
_____   **13.** Supporting documents
_____   **14.** On financial statements
_____   **15.** A liability

a. Purchase order
b. Vouchers Payable
c. Basis for recording voucher into voucher register
d. New voucher for each installment
e. Attached to vouchers
f. Invoices recorded at net
g. Varies from company to company
h. After paid
i. Prepared at end of month
j. Unpaid voucher file
k. Voucher system
l. Dr. Vouchers Payable; Cr. Vouchers Payable, and Purch. Ret. and Allow.
m. Accounts Payable replaces Vouchers Payable
n. Credit balance
o. Check register

Part III Instructions

Answer true or false to the following.

1. A voucher system cannot control a company's cash payments.
2. The invoice should never be compared to a purchase order or a purchase requisition.
3. Supporting documents should not be attached to the original voucher.
4. The account distribution on an invoice indicates to which account(s) the invoice should be charged (as a debit).
5. Vouchers are entered into the voucher register in alphabetical order.
6. The term Accounts Payable may be used on financial statements instead of the term Vouchers Payable.
7. A tickler file is really an unpaid voucher file.
8. The unpaid voucher file is really like a subsidiary ledger.
9. Checks are listed in a check register in alphabetical order.
10. Vouchers, after being paid, should be kept for no more than three years.
11. The normal balance of Vouchers Payable is a credit.
12. The purchases journal in a voucher system is needed along with a voucher register.
13. Vouchers can be cancelled.
14. Invoices recorded at gross means there is a need for an account called Discounts Lost.
15. Discounts Lost is an asset account.
16. A cash payments journal is not needed in a voucher system.
17. A voucher register is a supplementary record.
18. Vouchers are prepared for each installment if paid in partial payments.
19. Vouchers are defaced when recorded in the voucher register.
20. A voucher system is really an external control system.

CHAPTER 23
SOLUTIONS TO SUMMARY PRACTICE TEST

Part I

1. voucher system
2. voucher
3. purchase order
4. accounting department
5. numerical order
6. unpaid voucher file
7. Vouchers Payable
8. check register
9. sequential order
10. schedule of vouchers payable
11. Discounts Lost
12. Purchases Discounts
13. cancelled
14. credit
15. accounts payable ledger

Part II

1. f
2. a
3. h
4. k
5. c
6. i
7. n
8. l
9. o
10. d
11. g
12. j
13. e
14. m
15. b

Part III

1. false
2. true
3. false
4. true
5. false
6. true
7. true
8. true
9. false
10. false
11. true
12. false
13. true
14. false
15. false
16. true
17. false
18. true
19. false
20. false

DEPARTMENTAL ACCOUNTING

INSTANT REPLAY: SELF-REVIEW QUIZ 24-1

1. _____ 2. _____ 3. _____

INSTANT REPLAY: SELF-REVIEW QUIZ 24-2

DEPT. A	DEPT. B

INSTANT REPLAY: SELF-REVIEW QUIZ 24-3

1. _____ 2. _____ 3. _____ 4. _____ 5. _____

CONCEPT CHECK

1.   Toys   Clothing

_____

_____

_____

2.

_____

_____

_____

_____

3.

Net Sales   _____
  − Cost of Goods Sold   _____
  = Gross Profit on Sales   _____
  − Operating Expenses   _____
     Income Before Taxes   _____
  − Income Tax Expense   _____
     Net Income   _____

4.

		DEPT. A		DEPT. B		TOTAL	

CONCEPT CHECK (CONCLUDED)

5.

		DEPT. A		DEPT. B		TOTAL	

FORMS FOR EXERCISES A OR B

24A-1 OR 24B-1

Jewelry   Hardware   Automotive

_____

_____

_____

24A-2 OR 24B-2

A.   B.   C.

_____

_____

_____

24A-3 OR 24B-3

   Net Sales _____

  − Cost of Goods Sold _____

  = Gross Profit on Sales _____

  − Operating Expenses _____

   Income Before Taxes _____

  − Income Tax Expense _____

   Net Income _____

24A-4 OR 24B-4

	DEPT. A	DEPT. B	TOTAL

EXERCISES (CONCLUDED)

24A-5 OR 24B-5

		DEPT. A		DEPT. B		TOTAL	

END OF CHAPTER PROBLEMS

PROBLEM 24A-1 OR PROBLEM 24B-1

ACCELERATED STOP
INCOME STATEMENT SHOWING DEPARTMENTAL GROSS PROFIT
FOR YEAR ENDED DECEMBER 31, 20X9

PROBLEM 24A-1 OR PROBLEM 24B-1 (CONCLUDED)

ACCELERATED STOP
INCOME STATEMENT SHOWING DEPARTMENTAL GROSS PROFIT
FOR YEAR ENDED DECEMBER 31, 20X9

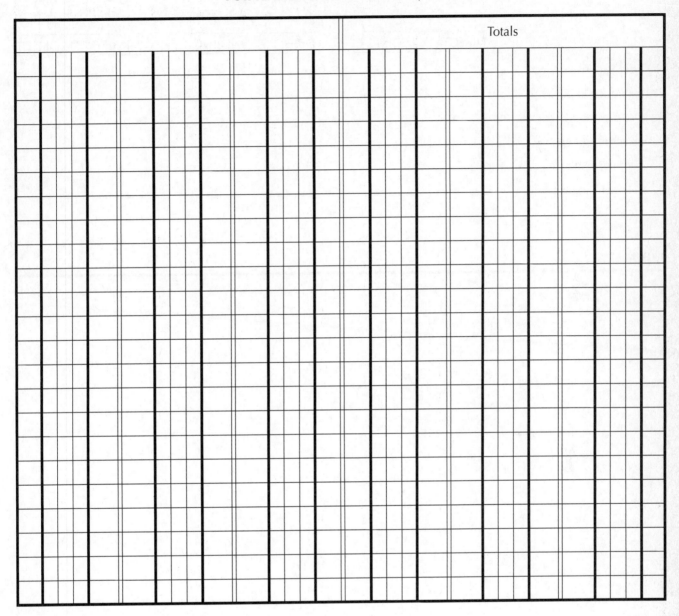

Totals

PROBLEM 24A-2 OR PROBLEM 24B-2

DEPARTMENTAL EXPENSES

					TOTAL OPERATING EXPENSE	
	DIRECT	INDIRECT	DIRECT	INDIRECT	DIRECT	INDIRECT
1. Rent Expense						
2. Insurance Expense						
3. Depreciation Expense						
4. Advertising Expense						
5. Supplies Expense						
6. Salaries Expense						

Work Area

PROBLEM 24A-3 OR PROBLEM 24B-3

INCOME STATEMENT SHOWING DEPARTMENTAL INCOME BEFORE TAX
FOR YEAR ENDED DECEMBER 31, 20X9

TOTALS

PROBLEM 24A-4 OR PROBLEM 24B-4

DEPARTMENTAL EXPENSES

(1)	DIRECT	INDIRECT	DIRECT	INDIRECT	TOTALS
A. Salaries Expense					
B. Depreciation Expense					
C. Advertising Expense					
D. Administrative Expense					
E. Rent Expense					

Work Area

PROBLEM 24A-4 OR PROBLEM 24B-4 (CONCLUDED)

INCOME STATEMENT SHOWING DEPARTMENTAL CONTRIBUTIONS
TO INDIRECT EXPENSE NOVEMBER 30, 20X9

(2)   TOTALS

CHAPTER 24
SUMMARY PRACTICE TEST:
DEPARTMENTAL ACCOUNTING

Part I Instructions

Fill in the blank(s) to complete the statement.

1. A(n) _____ _____ is a unit that allows a manager the responsibility of controlling and incurring costs as well as generating revenue.

2. A unit in which the manager has no control in generating revenue but does control and incur costs is called a(n) _____ _____.

3. Operating expenses that can be traced and identified directly to a department are called _____ _____.

4. _____ _____ are operating expenses that cannot be identified to a specific department but are incurred on behalf of the company.

5. In departmental accounting, separate _____ can be established for each department.

6. Gross profit is equal to net sales less _____ _____ _____ _____.

7. A direct expense for one company could be a(n) _____ _____ for another company.

8. Indirect expenses might be allocated on the basis of _____ _____ that each department occupies.

9. Indirect expenses may be allocated for each department based on _____ sales.

10. Allocating indirect expenses can be somewhat _____.

11. Gross profit less _____ _____ equals income before taxes.

12. Departmental _____ to indirect expenses result in indirect expenses not being combined with direct expenses.

13. Gross profit on sales less _____ _____ expenses equals contribution to indirect expenses.

14. An income statement showing _____ _____ before tax lists the operating expenses (both direct and indirect) for each department.

15. Operating expenses can be direct, indirect, or _____ both.

Part II Instructions

Match the term in the column on the left to the definition, example, or phrase in the column on the right. Be sure to use a letter only once.

__j__	**1.** EXAMPLE: Cost center	a. Incurs costs and generates revenue
_____	**2.** Departmental expense sheet	b. Net sales less cost of goods sold
_____	**3.** Debate about indirect expenses	c. Traced directly to a specific department
_____	**4.** The computer	d. Allocation of an indirect expense
_____	**5.** Indirect expenses	e. Could be arbitrary
_____	**6.** Profit center	f. Gross profit less operating expenses
_____	**7.** Gross profit	g. Worksheet allocating direct and indirect expenses
_____	**8.** Contribution to indirect expenses	h. May require some judgmental decisions
_____	**9.** Income before taxes	i. Could gather departmental information
_____	**10.** Direct expenses	j. Incurs costs but does not generate revenue
_____	**11.** Gross profit minus direct departmental expenses	k. Hard to control by manager
		l. Cannot be traced to a specific department
_____	**12.** The allocation process of indirect expenses	m. Used to calculate gross profit
		n. Contribution to indirect expenses
_____	**13.** Separate accounts for each department	o. Gross profit less direct departmental expenses
_____	**14.** Space reduction of one department	
_____	**15.** Based on square footage	

Part III Instructions

Answer true or false to the following.

1. A profit center and a cost center are the same thing.
2. A direct expense for one company could never be an indirect expense for another company.
3. A manager of a cost center can generate revenues.
4. Special journals add to posting labor when several departments are involved.
5. Each department must have its own special accounts for cost of goods sold.
6. Net sales plus cost of goods sold equals gross profit.
7. Gross profit plus direct expenses equals net sales.
8. All operating expenses are indirect expenses.
9. Operating expenses are listed on the balance sheet.
10. Allocation of operating expenses is not subjective.
11. Sales salaries may be a direct expense for a company.
12. Allocation of indirect expenses may not consider the position of space for a specific department.
13. Depreciation expenses can be an indirect expense.
14. Allocation of indirect expenses can be based on gross sales.

15. Indirect expenses can be allocated based on square footage.
16. Direct departmental expenses are traceable to a specific department.
17. Gross profit on sales less total direct departmental expenses equals contribution to indirect expenses.
18. Contributions to indirect expenses less indirect departmental expenses equals gross profit.
19. Trends in industry may affect which departments might be expanded or contracted.
20. Operating expenses can be direct, indirect, or partially both.

CHAPTER 24
SOLUTIONS TO SUMMARY PRACTICE TEST

Part I

1. profit center
2. cost center
3. direct expenses
4. Indirect expenses
5. accounts
6. cost of goods sold
7. indirect expense
8. square feet
9. gross
10. arbitrary
11. operating expenses
12. contributions
13. direct departmental
14. departmental income
15. partially

Part II

1. j
2. g
3. k
4. i
5. l
6. a
7. b
8. o
9. f
10. c
11. n
12. e
13. m
14. h
15. d

Part III

1. false
2. false
3. false
4. false
5. true
6. false
7. false
8. false
9. false
10. false
11. true
12. true
13. true
14. true
15. true
16. true
17. true
18. false
19. true
20. true

MANUFACTURING ACCOUNTING

Name _____ Class _____ Date _____

INSTANT REPLAY: SELF-REVIEW QUIZ 25-1

_____

_____

_____

INSTANT REPLAY: SELF-REVIEW QUIZ 25-2

GENERAL JOURNAL

PAGE 1

Date	Account Titles and Description	PR	Dr.	Cr.

INSTANT REPLAY: SELF-REVIEW QUIZ 25-3

1. _____ 2. _____ 3. _____ 4. _____

Name _____ Class _____ Date _____

CONCEPT CHECK

1.

A. _____

B. _____

C. _____

D. _____

2.

_____

_____

_____

_____

_____

3.

_____

_____

_____

_____

_____

_____

_____

4.

5. A. _____ B. _____ C. _____ D. _____

FORMS FOR EXERCISES A OR B

25A-1 OR 25B-1

A. _____

B. _____

C. _____

D. _____

25A-2 OR 25B-2

_____

_____

_____

_____

_____

25A-3 OR 25B-3

_____

_____

_____

_____

_____

_____

_____

25A-4 OR 25B-4

25A-5 OR 25B-5 A. Ending

Account	Dr. or Cr. Column	Section of the Worksheet
Raw Materials		
Goods-in-Process		
Finished Goods		

B. Beginning

Account	Dr. or Cr. Column	Section of the Worksheet
Raw Materials		
Goods-in-Process		
Finished Goods		

Name _____ Class _____ Date _____

END OF CHAPTER PROBLEMS

PROBLEM 25A-1 OR PROBLEM 25B-1

JENNINGS MANUFACTURING
STATEMENT OF COST OF GOODS MANUFACTURED
FOR THE MONTH ENDED MARCH 31, 201X

PROBLEM 25A-2 OR PROBLEM 25B-2

KNIGHT MANUFACTURING
GENERAL JOURNAL

Date	Account Titles and Description	PR	Dr.	Cr.

PROBLEM 25A-3 OR PROBLEM 25B-3: Use one of the foldout worksheets that accompanied your textbook.

CHAPTER 25
SUMMARY PRACTICE TEST:
MANUFACTURING ACCOUNTING

Part I Instructions

Fill in the blank(s) to complete the following statements.

1. The _____ _____ is completed before the cost of goods manufactured is prepared.

2. The three major inventories are _____ _____, work-in-process, and _____ _____.

3. Overhead may be applied based on _____ _____ hours.

4. A(n) _____ _____ _____ is issued to the carrier of the finished product.

5. The worksheet shows a figure for cost of _____ _____ for a manufacturing company.

6. _____ _____ shows movement of materials or products between departments.

Part II Instructions

Match the term in the column on the left with the definition, example, or phrase in the column on the right. Be sure to use a letter only once.

__b__   1.   EXAMPLE: Bill of lading
_____   2.   Receiving report
_____   3.   Directly related
_____   4.   Retained Earnings
_____   5.   Manufacturing overhead
_____   6.   Overhead—Control
_____   7.   Work-in-process
_____   8.   Raw materials
_____   9.   Inventories
_____ 10.   Cost of goods manufactured

a. Manufacturing costs less raw materials and direct labor
b. Formal document
c. Credit column on income statement section of worksheet
d. Depreciation
e. Evidence of receipt of goods by receiving department
f. Processed into finished product
g. Raw materials, work-in-process, finished goods
h. Direct labor
i. Transfers to finished goods
j. Credit balance

Part III Instructions

Answer true or false to the following.

1. A bill of lading is a formal document that is issued to the carrier of the finished product.
2. Wages directly affect the quality, color, or other characteristics of the products.
3. The figure for cost of goods manufactured is usually placed in the credit column of the income statement on the worksheet.
4. The statement of costs of goods manufactured lists finished goods.
5. The ending balances of raw materials inventory and work-in-process are entered in the credit columns of the cost of goods manufactured on the worksheet.
6. Inventories on a balance sheet are made up of raw materials, work-in-process, and finished goods.

CHAPTER 25
SOLUTIONS TO SUMMARY PRACTICE TEST

Part I

1. income statement
2. raw materials, finished goods
3. direct labor
4. bill of lading
5. goods manufactured
6. Lot ticket

Part II

1. b
2. e
3. h
4. j
5. a
6. d
7. i
8. f
9. g
10. c

Part III

1. true
2. true
3. false
4. false
5. true
6. true